Thomas Hampson

History of Rivington

Thomas Hampson

History of Rivington

ISBN/EAN: 9783741155888

Manufactured in Europe, USA, Canada, Australia, Japa

Cover: Foto ©ninafisch / pixelio.de

Manufactured and distributed by brebook publishing software (www.brebook.com)

Thomas Hampson

History of Rivington

HISTORY
OF
RIVINGTON

WITH
LISTS OF THE CLERGY AND CHURCHWARDENS,
THE CHURCHWARDENS' ACCOUNTS,
PARTICULARS OF THE RIVINGTON AND BLACKROD
GRAMMAR SCHOOLS,
AN ACCOUNT OF THE PILKINGTON FAMILY,
&c., &c.

AND COPIOUS INDEX.

BY
THOMAS HAMPSON,
Author of "History of Horwich," "History of Blackrod,"
"Horwich Legends," &c.

WIGAN:
ROGER & RENNICK, 19, Market Street.
HORWICH:
"Chronicle" Office.
1893.

DEDICATORY.

Respectfully inscribed by kind permission to Richard Shaw, Esq., Gilsbrook, Rivington, as the representative of one of the most ancient of Rivington Families; and as an acknowledgment of the valuable aid rendered in the compilation of this contribution to Local History by his humble Servant, the Author,

THOMAS HAMPSON.

LEE LANE,
    HORWICH, 1893.

HISTORY OF RIVINGTON.

CHAPTER I.

"Sweet Rivington, or Riventon, thou art a lovely place,
In every hill, in every dale, some beauty we may trace."

* * * * * *

"When Rivington puts on her hood
   She fears a rainy day,
But when she doffs it you will find
   The rain is o'er, and still the wind
   And Phœbus shines away."

RIVINGTON, Rovington, Riventon, Rivenpike. Such are some of the ancient names that are now merged into that village of hill and lake, mountain and plain, into whose history, legends, and time-honoured cock-crowned church, we purpose, in the range of these papers, to enter. History verily cannot be written, it can only be copied. We may change its dress, and alter its habiliments and surroundings, cast aside its ancient, antiquated *personnel*, but in whatever form the change may appear, in whatever aspect the metamorphosis may strike the eye, there must remain the original bust, and though cloaked by traditions, and surrounded and almost lost in the "folk lore" of a bye-gone age, yet as we cast away one by one these additions, which repeated periods have given, we may perchance in a more modest, and simple manner, like Layard at Nineveh, by digging and upheaving, find some pristine gem, unveil some lost sign, and in loch, wood, hill, and glen, discover some caligraphic sign that may guide our investigations, or some hieroglyphic that may lead to success. Few, if any portions of the districts in the County Palatine are so rich in those traditions that throw a holy halo, and nurture a sympathetic interest in the bye-gones of history, as is this picturesque and lovely village, that seems ever resting in calm repose under the shade of "the everlasting hills." Thousands mount its rugged slopes year by year, and enter its tortuous glens, drink from its rippling streams, and are baptized afresh with the spray of its waterfalls. They fight heroically against the prickly gorse and treacherous brushwood; they mount its cliffs, and clap their hands at the dawn of beauty that breaks on their vision. The enchantment lends enthusiasm to the poetic aspect, and the eye alone is gratified. "Italy," said a writer, who had passed a great portion of his time in that lovely region, "may have summer skies and beautiful landscapes; but none could beat the one I was favoured with on my first visit to that lovely Lakeland," and certainly under favourable conditions, when "Jupiter Pluvius" forgets his spite against Lancashire, and dries up his tears, no spot could be more exhilarating, no air more impregnated with lung-reviving energy and health-giving properties than that of "Sweet Rivington."

Rivington, so far as the memory of that mystic individual—the oldest inhabitant—goes, has been a place in which pleasure seekers and those who delight to "drink in Nature's beauties" have always delighted to roam; and its traditions have a fascinating influence on the imagination, and its history has a field of delightful research for the historian. Yea, the keen student, of whatever grade, may worship in its temple, and kneel before the "gods" as he bends to seek inspiration in its rocky glens and moss covered solitudes. The geologist, as he views its mountains of silent rock, draws whispers of consolation, and each step to him is fruitful of interest and redolent of the grand and awe inspiring truths which his loved science inculcates. On its wild moorland borders are lead mines of historic note; on its lofty tableland the "black diamond," coal, glitters almost to the surface, and "mountain mine" of the more fruitful coal districts has long added value to its heather-covered slopes. In mineral wealth the "Village of the Lakes" far surpasses its not ill-favoured neighbours, while its rocky cliffs and silent glens abound with the old red sandstone and granite-like deposits, which a Hugh Miller would have delighted to study. Yea, hidden beneath its swamps and emerald patches, where the bitter buxbaum, as it is called in the neighbourhood, luxuriates, is a bottled store of nature's fluid that will ere long be tapped for the use of the surrounding districts. In fact, as a mining engineer well known and highly respected in this neighbourhood—Mr. John Unsworth, of Scotlane Colliery, has said—"A sprig bit could scarcely be pricked into those hills without drawing water." But as we proceed on our imaginary journey we shall conduct our readers—

> Up by the mountain's rugged side
> To hear the rock-man in dreary glen,
> To view the landscape far and wide,
> Far from the busy haunts of men.

Rover, or Riven, both meaning to wander, carry us back in its etymology to a period when the class of people who would inhabit a district contiguous to the extensive forest at Horwich, and who were subject to a tyrannical supervision that was both galling and despotic, would be more or less of a normal characteristic, living in the fastnesses of the "Pike," protected by its intricate glens, and possessed of a power of watching the movements of any effort to disturb or molest them that might be made by the foresters, or their chief, with his armed retainers who perchance lay concealed in the swooping valley and extensive forest at Horwich.

The inhabitants of Rivington at this early period were doubtless more of the Saxon type, if not directly by consanguinity with the early Britons, and to them the forest laws, as promulgated by the Norman Conquerors, would be most tantalising and irritating. Even those who had dwelt more immediately on the borders of the forest, or perchance within its range, with the increased power of the rangers of the forest and the cruel laws which protected the denizens thereof, would be driven from within its borders; and what spot so dear, what position so good for those who cast an envying eye, as the rocky slopes, the gorse covered hills and fastnesses of the overhanging Pike, as a post of observation and survey? These wanderers, or rovers, feeling that they had been deprived of what they would consider much as a kind of hereditary right, would doubtless cast longing eyes upon that extensive and vast forest which had provided for their needs in days gone by. Rivington, by virtue of its fastnesses and its rocky glens, would not only be a sure protection, but its vast range of hills would also prove a grand point of observation. The agistments would prove a terrible and exacting law to those who, doubtless, previous to the haughty Norman claiming the common lands of the country, had been able to send their cattle and swine to feed within the extensive forest range. Driven thus from within the forest range, denied of the privileges of yore, these ancient occupiers of the forest boundary would become as Nomads, wandering amongst the cliffs and sheltering in the glens that abounded in the neighbourhood. History has already fully recorded the iniquity and the tyranny of these forest laws, and for a people such as the aborigines of Rivington, breathing a free air, claiming free rights, and exercising free privileges, to be thus ruthlessly deprived of immemorial rights by the vassals of a foreign conqueror, would evoke a spirit of opposition and rouse the lambent flame of local patriotism to its fullest development. Not only were they "riven" from their ancient rights, but they were also called upon in certain seasons to aid the foresters and acknowledge the yoke that bound them. Under such conditions the wild moorland would be their home, the treacherous morass their protection, the overhanging hills their point of observation, and the foresters their bitterest foes.

CHAPTER II.

Rivington Pike, and Roscoe Low,
Windy Runnets, and th' house below.

AT certain seasons of the year, the villagers of Lostock, Rumworth, Heaton, Halliwell, Sharples, and Anderton were called together in order that they might form a kind of cordon in protecting the forest in the most delicate and trying seasons. The animal—man—might decrease, but the denizens of the forest must needs increase and multiply. In the summary of the townships called upon to assist in the performance of this duty, in none of the old writings is there any mention of Rivington being thus taxed for the protection of this vast baronial forest. In the districts named, the male portion of the inhabitants were called upon to assemble, under heavy penalties, and were enrolled much in the manner of special constables. And no doubt this call was more imperative because upon its very borders there dwelt those who by virtue of ancient right, claimed to have some "part or lot" in those forest glades, and some share in that "food for man" which, at that period, such forests most abundantly provided. The ancient inhabitants of Rivington rebelled against these laws, and in true gipsy fashion took upon themselves those privileges that were denied them by the fiat of the proud baron who claimed sovereignty over the wild domain. One glance at these laws, propagated by the Norman barons, will be sufficient to show that a people accustomed to rural freedom could ill brook the tantalising and autocratic sway of the Norman purloiners of their ancient rights. In the season of the year when the hawks begin to build their nests, the inhabitants of the villages enumerated were commanded by those in charge of the forest to collect themselves in "Horewich-ley," and after being duly sworn and bound by oath, they were to go throughout the whole of the forest to see what nests they had made. To those border inhabitants of this wooded plain, who had been accustomed to look upon the denizens of the forest as their own, and who had ranged within its capacious shade, to be thus peremptorily denied of the sustenance it afforded, and the sport it provided, was very bitter, and, knowing, too, that the people who then held sway over it were those

> Who were allied to the Norman Will,
> Who came across the sea to kill,

there is no wonder at the opposition they offered, and the guerilla warfare they kept up, which, without increasing the brightness of their prospects, led to harsher measures, and more cruel laws.

That Rivington was a dependency of the Barony of Manchester there can be no doubt, though in the most ancient survey the name of the lord of Rivington does not occur. This, however, is no proof that Rivington was not included in the barony. According to Dr. Kuerden—and his view is confirmed by the "Testa de Nevill"—"Albert Gredley gave to Thomas de Perpoint three carucates of land in Ruthwinton and Lostoc by the fee of the third part of one knight," and "his heirs," says that document. "now hold the land." In the reign of Edward III. Rivington was enumerated among the fees of "Rogerus de Montebegon, baron of Hornby, near Lancaster, and then held of him by the Pilkingtons in thanage (Alexander Pakinton) Pilkington: ten v.j. bovates in Rovington in thanage, v. p. verve xxsp. annu. sed. portca.fil aronculi sin. teu. t.v.a. illam."(Baines.) These Pilkingtons were a family of great repute, not only in Lancashire, but also in Durham and other parts of the kingdom, and to this day they are associated with Rivington by ties treasured and strengthened the more the name of "good Bishop Pilkington" and his local patriotism and high character are studied. But in a future chapter we shall have to deal more especially with the divine who enriched Rivington, not only by the lustre of his exalted and noble character, but by the making provision for its intellectual needs. As we proceed we shall have occasion to refer more particularly to a divine who was as closely associated with Rivington, both by ties of birth and sympathy, as Bishop Pilkington, when we refer to its time-honoured Grammar School.

The name of the Pilkington family is not only associated with the County Palatine, but also with the more stirring events of early history. In the "Testa de Nevill," William Fitz William is mentioned as holding "twelve bovates of land in thanage for 24 shillings in Ruthwinton." A branch of the Pilkingtons, who also were thanage holders in Bury, became

ERRATUM. THE PILKINGTON MOTTO.

On page 13 the motto on the Pilkington Crest, the "Man and Scythe," is given as "Now Then, Now Then." It should be "Now Thus, Now Thus." The Motto owes its origin to one of the ancestors of the Pilkington family who wished to appear as a mower, but as he held the scythe the wrong way his attention was drawn to the fact, when he immediately exclaimed "Now thus, now thus," reversing the scythe as he repeated the words.

principal proprietors and owners in Rivington, and few ancient families in Lancashire have left their mark more imperishably on the history of this rural district. As knights of renown the "Pylkingtons" were closely mixed up with the struggles, the battles, the victories, and defeats which alternately prevailed. And, though betimes wealth, power, and influence followed the sword, yet like many others in those delicate times, amidst the discord of faction, the march of ambition, and the anarchy of government, the Pilkingtons had their full share of both honour and disgrace. The terrible battle of Bosworth Field, in 1485 was pregnant with disastrous consequences to many noble houses, and not the least to that of the knightly Pilkingtons, who suffered almost as much in their fortunes as did their Sovereign in power and authority. In the grant made by Henry VII. to Thomas, Earl of Derby, of divers lands and premises in Lancashire, many of the principal centres of Lancashire are referred to. The property, however, in Rivington not belonging to Sir Thomas Pilkington escaped the wreckage. The Pilkingtons were long the Lords of the Manor of Rivington. Fuller says of the Pilkingtons, "They were gentlemen of repute in this shire (Lancashire) before the Conquest, and the chief of them was sought for after the battle of Harold with the Normans, in which the fortunes of Harold were dissipated. He was fain to disguise himself as a mower." It was in allusion to this circumstance that the "Man and scythe" were adopted as the family crest, with the motto "Now then, now then!" From Richard, second son of Sir Roger Pilkington, lord of Pilkington, descended Richard, lord of the manor of Rivington. He married Alice, daughter of Lawrence Asshawe, of the Hall-in-the-Hill, Heath Charnock. This Richard is more largely incorporated with the history of Rivington in its ecclesiastical aspect, he having built Rivington Church.

The Pilkingtons were of influence both in Church and State, and alike in the military affairs of the country, and in its ecclesiastical machinery, they were verily a power. James, his son, became famous as Master of St. John's College, Cambridge, and his theological knowledge, his standing as a divine of erudition and learning, gave him the exalted and honourable position "of being one of the six divines for correcting and compiling the Book of Common

Prayer" as used in the Church of England, for which service he was created Bishop of Durham. Bishop James Pilkington, B.D., first Protestant Prelate of the See of Durham, was the son of Richard Pilkington, of Rivington Hall, and was born in 1518. A plate at Stand near Prestwich, is inscribed "Bishop Pilkington, first Protestant Bishop of Durham, born in 1518." He was educated at St. John's, Cambridge, where it is supposed he took his D.D. degree. He became quite prominent in educational matters, and took a leading part in the movement then being made to revivify Greek literature in that ancient seat of learning. As a reward for his services he was presented by Edward 6th to the vicarage of Kendal. The Reformation had scarcely matured when the young King, who had so keenly taken up the Protestant cause, was called "To that bourne whence no traveller returns," and his successor to the throne soon began to show her predilection for the old faith. The Marian persecution began in all its harrowing bitterness—a bitterness, doubtless, intensified by the highhanded manner in which they who remained firm to the traditions of their fathers had been treated in the first fruits of Protestant rule. The country was torn in twain. Reprisals came swift and terrible. Some became exiles; others stayed behind to suffer. The fires of Smithfield illumined the country with their ghastly and cruel glare, and tribulation stalked through the land. During this period of anguish and sorrow, Bishop Pilkington was a voluntary exile in Geneva, and it was during this residence abroad that he imbibed those Calvinistic theories that came so prominently to the fore in more peaceful times. Mary, being called away from her earthly home, her sister Elizabeth, in whom centred the hope of the Protestant cause, was called to the Throne, and the voluntary exile, feeling assured that he would now be able to worship God in a way and manner agreeable to his conscience, once more landed on his native shore, and on June 20th, 1559, was elected Master of St. John's College, Cambridge. Honours came rapidly upon him, his scholastic and theological success being commensurate with his zeal; and, though a fearless preacher (as we shall have occasion to demonstrate) and devout divine, he nevertheless, though both the ecclesiastical and civil power fell under his denunciation, was called to the princely See of Durham, being consecrated on the 2nd of March, 1560, and enthroned on the 10th April following.

CHAPTER III.

BISHOP Pilkington was one of those heroes of history who exercised a judgment, sustained by careful enquiry and intelligent conviction. He was fearless in his utterances, and though betimes a warmth of expression, and a pungent use of words, are associated with him, yet there is the indelible sign of the man and the stamp of the Christian in those manly and fearless expressions, those candid warnings, and stern rebukes, from which even Royalty escaped not. "Good Queen Bess," who claimed in her own person to be the virtual "Head of the Church," as well as of the civil government, escaped not his scathing criticism, and his firm denunciation. The "Good Bishop" was no royal cringer. "Honour the King" was not a blind, servile command with him. Such great and dutiful respect was born from affection "to the powers that be" in so far as in their exalted places they rightly fulfilled their obligations. And the persistency of the Bishop was rewarded by Elizabeth making restitution of many valuable manors and estates, though she enriched the crown and many of her favoured parasites at the expense of the Church she claimed to love so dearly. But not even the warmth of the Bishop's condemnation, nor yet the grace and elegance of his appeal, could induce the virgin Queen to give up her spoils till an honorarium of £1,020—a large sum in those days—had been granted to the crown. From his exile Bishop Pilkington, as did many other divines of lesser note, brought back with him many vagaries of the Geneva School. He had imbibed a dislike to the cap and surplice of yore, and in a letter to the Earl of Leicester, dated "Auckland, 15th Oct., 1564," he points out "The delight of Papists to see the use of their apparel by Protestants, and affirms the surplice to be of an heretical spring." In 1564 Bishop Pilkington paid a visit to his Cathedral at Durham, complained to his Archbishop of the then existing state of spiritual matters in the North, and condemned those in authority in the Church for being lethargic and easy. He brings proof of his assertions. His Episcopalian brother of Chester is charged with indifference to his spiritual functions, and his neglect of a due visitation of his diocese, and with having compounded with the Archbishop of York for the omission. In this charge the spiritual life of the Church is reflected in a light that testifies to the want of godly vitality, and the disruptions that "rent in twain the temple" were born and nurtured by this indifference to the most holy and exalted duties.

To those who look upon the mighty schisms that have from time to time weakened the "bond of unity" in the Christian Church, and who deplore the existence of errors in the grand tabernacle designed by the Carpenter's Son, there is presented to the secular eye disjointed, and in many instances opposing forces, and they find the seeds of this breach, alas, too often sown by those who in the most solemn form have taken the oath of allegiance and sworn fidelity to the great trust reposed in their hands. Bishop Pilkington traces "the gross indifference of the inferior clergy" to this supineness of the episcopal order, and the abuses which the Reformation was supposed to have rooted out were again rising to the surface. Not only was this indifference manifested in absenting themselves from the sphere of their spiritual labours, but it also displayed itself in the mode and manner of divine service. "It is lamentable," says the pious Bishop, "to see and hear how negligently they say divine service," and he plainly tells the Archbishop that "Your cures, all except Rochdale, be as far out of order as the worst in the country. The old Vicar of Blackburn resigned for a pension. Whalley hath as ill a vicar as the worst; and there has one come thither that hath been deprived or changed his name. The Bishop of Man liveth here at ease, and as merry as Pope Joan. The Bishop of Chester hath compounded with my Lord of York for his visitation, and gathered up the money by his servants, but never a word spoken of any visitation or reformation." This was characteristic of such a noble prelate as Bishop Pilkington, and the spot that can claim him as one of its sons must be honoured in having such a name on its imperishable scroll. But how far this honour has been exercised we shall have occasion to refer as we proceed.

On the 8th of June, 1565, he preached a remarkable sermon at St. Paul's Cross, on the burning of St. Paul's Cathedral, exhorting the people to take the event as a warning of greater plagues yet to follow, if amendment of life was not made in all estates. His occupancy of the See of Durham was not altogether a bed of roses. The gathering clouds had, for some time past, cast their threatening shadows before them. In Church and in State the volcano only slumbered; the dreadful omens had already darted across the horizon; the storm bird had uttered its weird cry; and a tone of distrust, a harbinger of coming peril, was seen by those who studied the signs of the times. Religious disturbances had broken out in the North. The principles, the polity, and wisdom of the Reformation were discussed. The subversion of the great work of that historic period was threatened, and surrounding high places the spirit of distrust and a feeling of danger were engendered. The authority of the civil power was in danger, and the destruction of civil government imminent. A powerful nobleman of the highest hereditary claims, the premier Duke of Norfolk, had aspired to the hand of the Queen of Scots, and this, in the tension and excitement inseparable from religious feuds, conjured up a danger to the existing constitution as great as if a foreign invader was preparing a descent upon our shores. The historical incidents of this period are so well-known by their tragic surroundings that it is unnecessary further to pursue them, only so far as they are connected with Rivington's Bishop —Son. The avaricious spirit of Elizabeth was aroused, vast estates were sequestered. The minions at her court were enriched by the spoils, and impecunious noblemen fattened on their brother's loss, the sordid Queen, however, looking well to her own needs. The country was in an unsettled state, disturbances broke out hither and thither, and as a matter of prudence, and not because of any individual activity in the turmoil, Bishop Pilkington, being a married man, retired, and died at Auckland on the 23rd of January, 1575, and was there interred. His remains, however, were afterwards removed to Durham, and re-interred in the Cathedral Choir.

Bishop Pilkington, as the founder and endower of the Old Grammar School at Rivington, is best known, locally, through that endowment, and so long as Rivington shall last his name will be associated with it. The endowment of this school is gathered from lands and rents, almost exclusively in the first instance situate in the County of Durham, but owing to the distance from the school the endowment was meant to benefit, it was by power of Act of Parliament exchanged for lands, &c., more in the immediate neighbourhood of the school. The object of the Bishop was specified clearly "For the bringing, teaching, and instructing children and youth in grammar and other good learning, to continue for ever, and by the terms of the 'letters patent,' the school is open to all our faithful and liege people, whosoever therebe." But a mighty wave has swept away its grand privileges from those for whom they were intended, and those for whom this Pyrian spring was made to flow drink but little at its fountain. Doubtless the indifference to their weal by the more humble classes has much to answer for in the change. But in due order we shall have more to say in reference to the Elizabethan structure that now is so prominent an object to ramblers along Rivington-lane.

Bishop Pilkington adorned his "lawn sleeves" by his mental activity, and was a writer of no mean order. In a memoir of him by the Rev. J. Whittaker, M.A., we have some particular reference to the Bishop, and the work from which we quote is all the more interesting to us because it bears on the inside cover the "Ridgway Arms," and the name "Joseph Ridgway, Ridgmont." Here we are told that "James Pilkington, the founder of Rivington Grammar School, was born about the year 1520, the third son of Richard Pilkington, of Rivington, Esq., descended from the ancient and knightly family of the Pilkingtons of Pilkington, and Alice, his wife, daughter of Lawrence Asshawe, of the Hall-of-the-Hill, Heath Charnock. The house of his nativity was probably Rivington Hall, the principal residence of his father, situated in the picturesque and widely-extended valley at the north-west of Rivington Hill. As James Pilkington in after life filled important stations, and is spoken of by his contemporaries as a "learned person," it becomes a matter of some interest to inquire where the foundation was laid, which could bear in academical life so high a superstructure. The Grammar School of Manchester was then of recent foundation (founded by Hugh Oldham, LL.B., Bishop of Exeter, who is generally supposed to be a native of Oldham, and who died in 1520) and it is not improbable that some of the sons of Pilkington, who were designed for the church, received here the elements of their classical learning, or perhaps were pupils of the monks in some of the neighbouring religious houses ; the most celebrated being Whalley and Upholland. Whether Pilkington had been predisposed towards the Reformation, through paternal guidance, or like the greater portion of the old Lancashire families, had a preference for the faith of his fathers, we have no evidence to determine."

CHAPTER IV.

THE father of the famous Bishop had lived through the most changeful period of English Ecclesiastical History. He had seen the duplicity of the lustful Henry VIII., heard of his quarrel with the Pope, and seen the rival forces of the Civil and Ecclesiastical powers arrayed in opposition. In his later years he saw the youthful Edward swayed by Cranmer, and using his royal authority to back up a new faith, and a new method of Church government. The changes which the Reformation brought about would come fully before him. But how far the advent of the Reformation affected the Bishop's parent there is no guide. Doubtless the divine in embryo, with his keen perception, his active mental propensity, would early imbibe the doctrines of the new movement with his entrance into Cambridge University, where he heard the powerful preaching and teaching of Latimer, Ridley, and other stars of this period. The new doctrines permeated the most conservative of these ancient seats of learning, and Pembroke Hall became the focus around which the "new light" radiated. Around him were those who ere long sealed their adhesion to grand and noble principles by their blood; and the fires of Smithfield virtually singed the Bishop's coat. Whatever were the religious predilections of the senior Pilkington, there is no disputing the fact that the Bishop whose name is so intimately interwoven with Rivington early imbibed views peculiar to his surroundings. Ridley and Latimer had roused the slumbering volcano which had betimes given its warning within the classical precincts of a great University. In this scholastic nursery the signs were discerned that for a time were hidden from the prying eyes of vigilant ecclesiastics that were verily the beginning of that lambent flame that radiated and converged into that glorious epoch spoken of as the Reformation. Like other great and important changes that were destined to modify the current of religious opinion, the pioneers of the new movement found themselves saddled with a grave responsibility, and, though in an age when men were little accustomed to think for themselves and hoary traditions took the place of living faith, these worthies of the past were early called to champion their cause. Edward the 6th in the infancy of his reign had the bearing of this important change argued before him, and in a disputation which took place on Monday, the 24th of June, 1549, when the question was "In the Lord's Supper is none other oblation or sacrifice than one only remembrance of Christ's death and of thanksgiving," Pilkington was one of the disputants. At this time he was a Senior Fellow of St. John's, Cambridge, he having been elected on the 3rd of July, 1548, and his oratorical powers were doubtless the cause of his first preferment, for on the 26th of January, 1550, we gather from Dr. Whitaker's "Richmondshire" that he was presented by the King to the Vicarage of Kendal. Whether the active duties connected with his clerical preferment, denied him of those opportunities for study, that seemed to be a portion of his existence or not, the fact remains that one year only did he minister as the Vicar of Kendal, and once again we find him within the enclosure of academic life as a resident Fellow of Cambridge. This retirement from active clerical supervision came shortly after Pilkington had lost his father, who died on May 20th, 1551, at the ripe age of 65. For a period of years, Pilkington remained within the area of this ancient seat of learning—years that were marked by preludes that in a short period were destined to evoke a national sympathy. Religion was a fluctuating ideal. The doctrines, laws, and ceremonies prescribed one day were annulled the next. Men's minds were tempest-tossed. There was no guide to principles, no rule to faith. What was proclaimed one day was denounced the next, and men were called upon to obey this chaotic law under pains and penalties of a severe type. But thus early the Bible had become more generally studied, the corruptions associated with the old religion were comprehended, and no mortal hand could stay the mighty wave that was sweeping over the nation. The capricious tyranny and lewd designs of Henry had given place to a younger but a holier impulse, personified on the regal seat in the noble youth, Edward VI. Under his influence, and by his controlling power the Papal religion ceased to be the religion of the realm, and Protestantism, with little variation from its present form, became the acknowledged religion of the State, both in Crown and Commonwealth. Miles Coverdale had superintended the printing of the Bible at Zurich, and a royal edict had been issued to all the clergy commanding them to provide a book of the whole Bible both in Latin and English to be laid in the "quire" of the churches on or before the 1st of August, 1536, for every man that will loke and read thereon." The title page was as follows:—"Biblia, the Bible, that is the Holy Scriptures of the Olde and New Testament, faithfuly and truly translated out of the Douche and Latin into English, M.D., XXXV.," and on the last page we have these words: "Prynted in the yeare of our Lord, M.D., XXXV., and fynished the fourth daye of October." The fulsomeness of joy which heralded the ascension of the young king was nipped almost in the bud. The delicate health of the young sovereign cast its death shadow before it, and ere long the dread storm burst over a happy country, for with the death of Edward in 1553, the dark fears of the Protestants were more than realized. But these events are only incidental to our object, and possess under present consideration no affinity only as to the effect upon the Pilkington of Rivington. Stephen Gardiner, quondam Bishop of Winchester, had become Chancellor of the University, the statutes against heresy were revived, and John Christopherson, D.D., was authorized to exhibit the following three articles at Cambridge, and enjoin obedience to them : 1st. For the use of habits according to degrees. 2nd. For the pronunciation of Greek. 3rd. For the following titles of the king and queen to be mentioned by the preachers, Philip and Mary by the grace of God, king and queen of England, France, Naples, Jerusalem, and Ireland, Defenders of the Faith, Princes of Spaine and Sicill, Archduke of Austrich, Duk of Millaine, Burgundy, and Brabant, counties of Haspurge, Flander, and Tyroll." Pilkington, like another patriot of a later but not less important period, resolved to quit the kingdom, and unlike Cromwell succeeded, but under what condition, and whether attended by personal risk, we have no evidence to show.

CHAPTER V.

LIKE many other exiles for the faith they professed in this period of the troubled state of the religious community, Pilkington, far from home and Fatherland, found consolation in the fraternity and consolatory hope which buoyed up those by whom he was surrounded in that northern clime; and we find him mentioned as one of a party whom Bullinger, who had established a College at Zurich, cordially entertained. This collegiate chief felt deeply for them in the trials and troubles which had swept them from Albion's shores, and took energetic steps to evoke sympathy for them from those of influence and power. Surrounded by "friends in adversity," who had sought the same asylum, including Thomas Lever, a former Master of St. John's College, Pilkington found his exile not so galling as other conditions might have made it. And, in the fruition of those religious opinions and practices denied them at home, a ray of sunshine illumined their path. For a time the generosity of friends both at home and abroad was extended to them, and, as Humphreys, in his "Life of Jewel," remarks, "In retirement and diligent study, and in a blameless conversation, they laudably vied with each other in useful and honourable exercises." But even this aid from friends at home became precarious. Bishop Gardiner, whose name will ever be associated with the cruelties of the period, had intrigued himself into the highest position in the realm, and, as Lord High Chancellor of England, he wielded a power superior to the Throne itself, and took opportunity of his visit to the continent to learn something of the refugees, and, gathering that they were sustained by the contributions of their friends in England, his rancour against the Protestant section increased, and in the heat of his indignation, he declared that "the banished heretics should shortly be compelled to eat their own nails, and feed on their finger ends for very hunger." (Whittaker's Memoir.)

Troubles, however, grew apace, and we find Pilkington at Basle, where the more learned of the exiles were engaged in correcting the Press of a German named Operinus, who had undertaken the task of printing some of their publications. In the midst of their dark surroundings, a result which they had anticipated from the accounts they had received of Mary's health occurred; and most of the exiles at once set out to join in the national rejoicing at the accession of Queen Elizabeth. Pilkington, however, did not at once rush for the coast, for we find him at Frankfort in the beginning of January, 1559, and, on the third of that month he, along with others, subscribed to a letter sent from thence in answer to a circular addressed to the English residents on the continent. The letter breathes a spirit of conciliation, and is so pregnant with its broad and charitable views that perhaps even at the very advent of a great religious movement, a lesson of wisdom may be gathered that may be profitably studied at the present time. "As for ourselves, as we have had no contention with you at all aforetime, so we purpose not (as we trust there shall be no cause) to enter into contention with you hereafter. For ceremonies to contend, where it shall be neither in your hands nor ours to appoint what shall be; but in such men's wisdoms as shall be appointed to the devising of the same, and which shall be received by the common consent of Parliament, it shall be to small purpose. But we trust that both true religion shall be restored, and that we shall not be burdened with unprofitable ceremonies. And, therefore, as we purpose to submit ourselves to such orders as shall be established by authority, being not of themselves wicked, we would wish you willingly to do the same. For whereas all the reformed Churches differ among themselves in diverse ceremonies, and yet agree in the unity of doctrine, we see no inconvenience if we use some ceremonies diverse from them, so that we agree in the chief points of our religion."

In this extract we find the grand and glorious principle that governed the Reformers in their work; and, though undoubtedly the secular, rather than the religious, element in national life was more predisposed to the change which the Reformation brought to a result, yet throughout the whole range of English history the volcano had only slumbered, for the religion of this country in its earliest days was far removed from the abstract ceremonials of a later period. There was, however, a spirit of religious fervour pervading the minds of the Bishop and his co-exiles that might prove worthy of imitation in this boasted nineteenth century. "In the mean season let us, with one heart and mind, call to the Almighty God, that of His infinite mercy He will finish and establish the work that He hath begun in our country, and that we may lovingly consent together in the earnest setting forth of His truth, that God may be known and exalted, and his Church perfectly builded up through Christ our Lord."

Soon, however, Pilkington came to his native shore, and ere long he was in harness, for in the early part of February he appears as one of the compilers of that beautiful and incomparable Liturgy, which breathes the spirit of inspiration itself, and adorns the present ritual of the Church of England, with only slight modifications which the jealousies of an after period brought about. This new Liturgy had its enemies, and Pilkington was soon called upon to defend it from the attacks of those who not only questioned its legality, but also its adaptability and tenour. But Pilkington, in a pamphlet entitled "A defence of the English Service," aptly reminded them "that they had not acted more illegally in restoring their Liturgy than the former had done who had abolished one religion, legally established, and introduced another by force and violence"—a saying which places the learned Bishop amongst those who believe in the antiquity and continuity of the Church of England.

CHAPTER VI.

ONE of the expulsed Bishops of the Roman Church having privily written a little book to comfort his co-religionists in their distress, in whch he claimed the antiquity of that Church in England, Bishop Pilkington, as Stoype observes (vol. i., pp. 219-20), took cognisance of it, and in a work which he wrote concerning the burning of St. Paul's, "Offered to stand with him in the trial of this."

In the early part of 1562 we find Bishop Pilkington again in London, and, it may be presumed, attending to his legislative duties. This year was also memorable for the Convocation, or Synod, in which the Articles of Religion were revised and subscribed to. During the time the Bishop was in London, he preached before the Queen, in the month of June, presumably at St. Paul's Cross; and in his sermon he took occasion to expose a notorious imposter, who called himself Elias, and claimed the gift of prophecy. This prophet was a native of Manchester, and in the latter part of Queen Mary's reign, had played, with some success, on the credulity of the inhabitants; and so bold did he become in his claims that he ventured to 'wait upon her "Majesty" at the Royal Palace of Greenwich, pretending to have a message from God to deliver to her. On returning to his diocese, Bishop Pilkington found that the Roman Catholics had been endeavouring to seduce the people from their allegiance to the "Reformed Faith," and once again he came forward in defence of the Church for whose sake he had undergone such great tribulation. In a little book published under the title of "Common Good," he declared that it was "a labour undertaken for the sake of simple ones, that they should not be deceived and overcome with fond fancies of idle brains, and lest God's enemies should crack that none could or durst answer them."

Towards the end of the year 1563 rich patronage fell into the hands of the Bishop, and for two of his brothers he provided handsomely. He collated the elder of them, Leonard Pilkington, DD., Master of St. John's College, and Regius Professor of Divinity in the University of Cambridge, to the valuable Rectory of Whitburn, in the county of which he was the spiritual head. No sooner had he been able to show his brotherly affection in one direction, than opportunity offered itself for making his younger brother his Chaplain and Prebend of Durham in 1561.

This year was memorable for the Great Plague that visited not only the Metropolis, but assailed the whole country. The fears attending the Plague were intensified by shocks of earthquake, and the latter brought about the national call for a "day of humiliation and prayer." In a circular to the clergy the Bishop commanded an observance in the month of December. Prayers began in the Cathedral at Durham at six o'clock in the morning; at nine was the usual service; and again at three in the afternoon. Wednesdays and Fridays were kept as general fast days, with prayers and a sermon, and the services of the churches were in general better attended. (Stoype's Pathos, p. 135).

At this period it would be hard indeed to determine the exact position of the Church of England in relation to certain rites and ceremonies that she was supposed to have buried at the advent of the Reformation. In many places the only outward and visible sign was the substitution of the authority of the Queen for that of the Pope, and in what way the change had conduced to the benefit of the country it would be perplexing to say. There was really war within the borders of the Reformed Church, and to such an odious degree had controversies arisen that "the Reformation was beginning to be contemptible in the eyes of the public, and to afford an open triumph to the Papal party. Schism entered within her borders, and heresy broke out in her sacred precincts, till at length the Queen (perhaps from motives of policy) determined to enjoin Uniformity. The purlieus of the Court were besieged by interested partisans, and the services of influential persons were invoked." Bishop Pilkington wrote to Robert Dudley, Earl of Leicester, who, more from motives of policy than sympathy, had arrayed himself on the Puritan side. "I understand," said the Bishop, "by common reporte, and I fear too true, that there is grete offence taken with some of the ministrie for not using such apparel as the rest doe. Therefore, as in grete commen dangers of fire or such like, they that bee far off come to succure those that have need. So I, being out of that jeoparde and ferre off, cannot but of dutie wish wel to those that be touched in this case. I marvel much that this social controversie for apparel should be so heavily taken. Priests go with sword, dagger, and such course apparel as they can get, not being curious, or scrupulous, what colour or facion it be, and none is offended at them. But such grefe to be taken at a square cappe (which grete folie set on a round head) amonth theim that are civil, and ful of knowledge, is lamentable." The above letter was dated Auckland, the 25th Oct. 1564.

Bishop Pilkington might truly be termed the Liberal Bishop of the age, and though his letter made no impression at Court, and Archbishop Parker at the head of the Ecclesiastical Commission remained obdurate, how far the spirit which guided the Archbishop, and repeated in after days, has proved destructive in its effects on the Church of England we have no reason to inquire. The Queen herself was unwilling to listen to wise council, and an era of persecutions once more opened. Commissioners were appointed, and those who were "contumacious" were deprived. This action only strengthened the cause it was sought to injure, and accelerated the Puritan movement. In the beginning of March, 1565, Pilkington was again selected by the Lord Mayor of London as one of the preachers of the Spital Sermons at Easter, but Pilkington declined the honour. In this year he had the pleasurable satisfaction of a restitution of the lands that had been excepted out of his emoluments as a Bishop; and whether as a thanks offering, or as a token of that local patriotism which sometimes exercises so powerful an influence on the sympathies and feelings of individuals, he commenced the foundation of a school, which for some time previous he had contemplated for his native village of Rivington, a school, which, up to recent years, as we hereafter shall see, performed a useful function in giving a good and free classical education to those youths who availed themselves of its privileges.

Rivington would, no doubt, at this period, be often visited by the famous Bishop, as undoubtedly some portion of his family resided here, if not his mother herself. Around him, as he climbed its rugged slopes, or pierced its ravines, the associations of childhood and the exploits of youth would be recalled to memory. And after the dangers he had undergone, the vicissitudes through which he had passed, the stormy path he had travelled, what haven so sweet, what spot so dear, what more likely to draw out the deep benevolence of so noble a spirit, as the place which in

   Youth's golden dream he loved so well?

As the founder of Rivington Grammar School, Bishop Pilkington's name is best known to posterity, and in the union of the Rivington and Blackrod Grammar Schools, which we shall notice hereafter. Two historic names are associated under widely different aspects, and yet so contemporaneously as to merit a brief allusion. The last Warden of Manchester, previous to the Reformation, was Laurence Vaux, who was born at Blackrod, and no doubt received his early training at the old Grammar School at Manchester, and when the Reformation came, he, like Pilkington, was borne along with the torrent, and outwardly, at least, he joined the new order of things. But a dark day was approaching for some people, a day of tribulation and suffering; for others it was the welcome return of the "grand old faith" when the heralds told of Mary's accession to the Throne. The nation swayed with alternate joy and sorrow. To many a historic home it was a joyful harbinger—to others it was as the day of doom. No better illustration could be given of its general effects than that reflected in the action of the two men who have given a halo to their native villages. Pilkington, as we have already seen, "left home and fatherland" rather than deny the mighty impulse of a noble conscience, braving the perils that beseiged those who attempted to leave the country, and, across the wide seas, "bided God's good time." But Vaux returned to the fold, and on the death of Sir George Collyer, Warden of Manchester College, he became his successor. Vaux was born in Blackrod in the year 1526—a year rendered memorable as the one in which Luther publicly burned the "Pope's Bull," and the Pope as publicly excommunicated him. Thus the Rubicon was passed, the struggle begun.

CHAPTER VII.

ABOUT the time that Bishop Pilkington was elected Master of St. John's his name appears in the Commission for visiting the University. Almost one of the first acts of Queen Elizabeth's first Parliament had been to empower her Majesty to send Commissioners throughout all the dioceses to rectify the disordered condition into which the ecclesiastical machinery had fallen. Surrounding and pervading many of the churches were remnants of the adornment of the more Ritualistic Church of Rome, and the weak condition of the Church of England for remedying any defects in the body spiritual made it an incumbent case for the more powerful secular power to take action. Episcopal authority had not, as yet, regained its full strength and power, hence it was that a direct Commission was appointed. One important object of the Commission was to see that the registers were duly kept; that altars and images were removed and defaced, to administer the oath of supremacy, and to restore ejected ministers. Strype's Annals, vol. 1st, p. 167, say "Some of these had been deprived for religion, but the greatest number for marriage. Out of 16,000 of the inferior clergy, 12,000 were deprived or ejected in the reign of Queen Mary for entering into conjugal relations." And, if the report of the Commission be true, the morality of the English nation had not improved during the short period of Mary's reign, for, according to the presentments of the said Commission, "adultery, fornication, and illegitimacy" were met with in every parish.

The first public occasion on which Pilkington is mentioned as the select preacher before the University of Cambridge was somewhat remarkable. Two foreigners, Martin Bueer and Paulus Fagius, had been invited to England by the Archbishop of Canterbury (Cranmer), and, for a while, had shed a lustre over both Universities. Both of these two distinguished men soon, however, fell a prey to change of living and climate, and though their virtues were extolled, no public reference was made to them till the Virgin

Queen ascended the Throne. On the 30th July, 1560, a kind of funeral sermon was preached by James Pilkington, B.D., who selected his text from the 112th Psalm, and in this sermon the good divine took occasion to urge the necessity "of preferring none but men of principle and probity to stations of distinction and eminence in the Universities." In the Bodleian Library, at Oxford, is preserved his "Exposition of the prophesy of Haggai." Bishop Pilkington's first ordination after his appointment to the See of Durham was held on the 9th March, 1561, which was rendered the more remarkable in that he ordained on that occasion a relative, Richard Longworth, M.A., and a native of Bolton.

About the time that Bishop Pilkington had become resident in his diocese, and was enjoying alternate residence at his delightful castles of Auckland and Durham, he had married Alice, a daughter of one John Kingsmill, descended from the knightly family of the Kingsmills of Sidmanton, near Kingsclere, in Hampshire. The marriage of prelates was then unusual, and the Queen herself had a decided objection to such marriages. Hence it was that for a time, it is said, Pilkington kept his marriage secret. To the Roman Catholic party, who even then possessed no mean power both in Church and State, such marriages were really obnoxious, and often contentions of a violent nature occurred owing to this clerical privilege of being able to marry. In fact in Dr. Whittaker's "Life of Sandys," we are told that "to such a height was a contention of this kind carried on at Hartlebury, between the family of Dr. Sandys, Bishop of Worcester, and that of his Popish neighbour, Sir John Browne, that a great affray at length took place between the Bishop's servants and those of the Knight, and several were wounded."

Reference was made in our last chapter to the deep interest the Bishop had in Rivington, and to his determination to provide for its educational wants. In Lancashire, more perhaps than any county up to this period, the means of education had been most sparse, and from this cause the influence and object of the Reformation were declining in the County Palatine. This declension in so important a county caused the attention of those who had the interests of Protestantism at heart to turn their attention to education as the best remedy and the best agent for an extension of the Protestant cause. Even the Queen herself looked upon education as the impregnable barrier to the intrigues of Rome, and recommended it to her Council. Doubtless this action of his Royal patron, would rouse the enthusiasm of such a type as the Rivingtonian divine, and at once he set to work to obtain from the Queen, either by grant or purchase, the lands and out-rents with which he endowed his school at Rivington. The lands and rent charges which the Bishop appropriated for that purpose were originally situated at Lindake, Wolsingham, Wickham, Heighington, Stanhope, Stockton, Auckland, Silksworth, and Hetton-le-hole in the diocese of Durham, and were of the annual value of £30. But this original disposition of endowment has undergone a change since the legacies were granted, for many of them have been sold and other properties purchased in their stead more immediately in the neighbourhood of the school. Pilkington was successful in obtaining a charter, and by this charter of foundation these properties were vested in six governors, chosen from the six townships adjoining the school, who are incorporated governors of it, on condition that they pay to the master £20, and to the usher £10 yearly. The governors have the nomination to these two offices in their hands, but the appointments are really vested in St. John's, Cambridge, and the Bishops of Durham and Chester. As this act of beneficence was in a measure promoted by the money which the Queen had let loose and virtually brought into existence by her bounty, received her sanction, and established by her Royal Patent, the Bishop thought, doubtless, that it was only in justice that Elizabeth's name should be intimately connected with it, hence we find that he thought proper that it should be called "The Free Grammar School of Queen Elizabeth in Rovington, *alias* Rivington." The Queen's letters patent, establishing the foundation of the school, are dated the 13th of May, 1566, and in the course of that year it is said to have been opened. The statutes for the school, which the Bishop is said to have drawn up, were after a plan which his learned friend, Bernard Gilpin, M.A., had framed for the school which he founded and endowed at Houghton-le-Spring. These statutes, originally written in Latin, according to the custom of the age, point out in very minute and definite terms the plan and limitations of instruction contemplated by the Bishop. They contain also a precomposed form of prayers for the use of the school "which in their remarkable similarity of phraseology to the Liturgy of the Church, and the piety of their style, bear indubitable proofs of the hand that wrote them." At what period, or by whom the statutes were translated into English, cannot well be determined; but one of the old MS. bears date 1576.

Bishop Pilkington, though probably not a believer in Justinian's Code, would yet by his action seem to believe in its principle. This code is very precise, and, perhaps, with slight modifications, it would prohibit those "scandals" of the Church, which, even in these days of a crucible public opinion, betimes throw a dark shadow over its spiritual aspect. In Codicis I. tit. 3-42, we have the following: "It is therefore proper that those Priests should be chosen and ordained Bishops *who have neither children nor nephews*, for it is almost impossible that those who give themselves up to the cares of life which arise between children and parent, and which are of the very greatest importance, should spend all their thoughts and all their zeal on the service of God. For, since some pious persons, with the greatest hope in God, from an ardent desire of saving their souls, hasten to the churches, and bequeath to them all their worldly goods to the *use of the poor and indigent*, and for other pious purposes, it is highly improper that the Bishop should profit by them, or spend them on his own children and relations, *for a Bishop should be entirely free from all affections for children according to the flesh, that he may be the spiritual father of all the faithful.* On that account, therefore, we strictly forbid that anyone *having sons or nephews should* be ordained Bishops. Concerning those Bishops, however, who now are, or who shall be hereafter, we command that they should on no account have the power of leaving by will, or giving away (or by any other means that can be thought of) anything of their own property that they may have come in possession of, or acquired, *after they became Bishops*, either by will or donation, or any other manner, excepting only those things which they had before they were Bishops." If Bishops now-a-days were called upon to give account of their real and personal property before consecration, it would doubtless tend to that essential rule, that "Church property should be used for Church purposes," and private patronage would cease to work mischief on the body ecclesiastical, for throughout the country we have only 68 parishes where the right of electing the minister is vested in the inhabitants, and of these Rivington is one. But how far consistent with ecclesiastical polity this system may be, is perhaps open to grave doubts, when it is remembered that the licence to vote is given to those who can have no sympathy with a "Church by law established."

> Deeds of patriots may be forgot,
> In times of busy strife;
> But they are seeds that dieth not,
> But ever spring to life.

CHAPTER VIII.

We'll romp and skip, and have some fun,
And then to "Clock House" we will run.
For surely, lads, we'st catch it fine
If school we reach at after nine.

"Cock Thursday" comes with its hopes to-morrow,
To lads and lasses a joy or sorrow;
To aid your Master you're always willing
To bring this day the famous shilling.

THE will of Bishop Pilkington bears date the 4th February, 1571, and amongst other bequests to relatives and friends, he gave his books at Auckland to his brother Leonard, Rivington School, poor colleges and others; and from "Taylor's History, Merchant Taylors' School," we learn that one George Hart, a confessor in the reign of Queen Mary, an exhibition from the Bishop. In a second codicil he also bequeathed to his brothers George, Leonard, and John, everyone a silver pot-parcel gilt. To his nephew, Thomas Shaw, his sister Margaret, and his brother Francis the same. To Mr. Swift one of his best gowns. His wife and daughter were exccutrixes to his will, which was proved at York on the 18th Dec., 1576, by Alice Pilkington, otherwise Kingsmill. The Bishop himself was a branch of a very numerous family—seven sons, and five daughters. George, the second son, succeeded his father in the family estates in 1551, and in 1581 he was living at Rivington Hall. This George Pilkington by indenture made the 21st day of March, 23rd Eliz., devised and let to Robert Dewburst, M.A., master of the school, and his successors, the school-house at Rivington, for the term of 1,000 years, on condition of paying to himself, his heirs, and assigns, the sum of fourpence yearly, and a fine of two shillings at the end of every twenty-one years during that term. Of course nothing is now left of the ancient mansion of the Pilkington's. The old hall was said to have been built of wood and plaster, in the form of a quadrangle, enclosing within it a square court. This antiquated structure gave way to the improvements initiated by the predecessors of the present respected owner, J. W. Crompton, Esq., J.P., being pulled down in 1774, and the present red brick structure erected. In none of the great events of National History do the Pilkingtons play a part, and in the troubled times of the Civil Wars, they are chronicled not, and though doubtless from the antecedents that environ them, and the sympathies they had displayed at other stirring periods of historic note, they would be in keeping with the national aspiration, we are told that this seeming apathy was the result of an indenture "binding them not to take up arms against the King." The family records warned them of the great danger they incurred in being mixed up in quarrels so fickle in their results, for one of their ancestors had been attainted and beheaded by Henry VII., and his estates given to Thomas Stanley, created Earl of Derby. And only when another Earl of Derby sacrificed his life to his loyalty, another Pilkington purchased from the Parliamentary sequestrators a part of their ancient patrimony, a patrimony which had been lost to them for a period of two centuries. In the ninth year of James I. the executors of the Rivington estate sold it, and the name of Pilkington is only associated by history and tradition to that lovely rural spot. The statutes of the school, to which we referred in our last, bespeak a care and a culture that would almost deny the age. But in the historic ramble we oft come in contact with much that astonishes, and much that enhances our conception of those heroes of the past that have moulded and builded up the national character. "(First.) Every year once the Governours shall choose one of the discreetest and wisest of themselves to be Spokesman amongst themselves for that year, whose authority shall be to warn and call the rest of the Governours together at some convenient place and time, to debate, talk, and take orders for doing of such things as he himself of his own knowledge, or by the information of others, shall think meet to be done for the good governance of the school, or anything concerning it; and when his year is ended they shall choose him again, or some other sober, wise man of themselves, to do the like for the year following, and so continually for ever. Within one week after the year be ended that anyone hath been thus a Spokesman, or die within the year, the eldest Governour by election then being not sick and at home, shall call the rest of the Governours together for choosing another Spokesman for the year following; and likewise if the Spokesman be absent long at any one time of the year, or very sick that he cannot do his duty, and matters fall out necessary to be talked of or done by the Governours, the eldest by election being at home and not sick shall have like place and power to call the rest together for the doing and debating of such matters; and that which four (4) of them agree to, and others that are required thereunto according to these Statutes shall be good, and obeyed of the rest." The "Spokesman" referred to was an important personage, and he was so far surrounded with the insignia of his office as to convey to his mind, not only its attendant immediate duties, but by oath, this responsibility was more carefully riveted. "I. A. B., chosen to be a Spokesman for this year, of this School of Rivington, shall to the utmost of my power, study, foresee, and take care for such things as touch the commodity and good order of this school; and, allowed by James Pilkington, Bishop of Durham, I shall diligently see kept, so far as in me lieth, and when I shall know anything by myself, or by the information of others, that is doubtful and necessary, and toucheth the good order and statutes and profit of this school, I shall call my fellow governours together, and quietly debate the matter with them, and that which shall be agreed on by the most part of them according unto these statutes, I shall diligently put in execution to my power. So help me God." "If this spokesman do not his duty accordingly herein as he ought to do, or being warned will not amend his negligence quickly, the rest of the governours, or the most part of them, by the appointment of the eldest governour by election, may assemble themselves and choose another discreet man as afore was said to supply that town; and if any of the governours come not to the place, and at the time appointed, where he is warned to be by the spokesman, or his deputy, for any matter touching this school, he shall forfeit two shillings for every time that he is absent to the use of the school (except his cause be allowed by the most part of the governours), and he continue disobedient they may choose another in his place. When they be thus come together, which is to be wished to be in the Church, if it may be, their spokesman, or else his deputy, shall declare unto them the cause of their meeting and the matters that are to be done. The rest shall quietly hear, and every man shall freely, without blame, say his mind. And that which four of them agree on shall be done and obeyed of all the rest, except they will stand and prove it hurtful to the school or contrary to the orders made now by the governours, and allowed by James Pilkington, Bishop of Durham, and he that frowardly disobeyeth anything agreed on by the more part of the governours, according to the statutes, shall be corrected as the most part of them shall think meet, or else be no longer a governour. Everyone shall speak in the order as he is appointed a governour, the eldest that hath been longest governour, or is appointed or named first in the Queen's grant, shall say his mind first, and so the rest in order; the others shall quietly hear each other's opinions without chiding or checking of any man. But before they begin to talk they shall call on God by prayer severally, everyone by himself, desiring God so to rule their minds that they may do those things that be for His glory and profit to His people. And if they meet for the choosing of a governour or schoolmaster they shall procure also an exhortation to be made by the schoolmaster or some other learned man to move them to consider deeply their duty and weighty cause they have to do, declaring to them what good may follow in choosing a good man, and what harm if they do not. After these things are done, and afore they go to choosing any officer of the school, the spokesman shall read openly among all the governours and others that have any voice to give in that matter, all that piece of the statute that toucheth such an election as they may be about to make, and he shall declare what quality and conditions he shall have that is to be chosen to that office, that they may the better thereby consider their duty, and keep their oath, which they must all take before they go to any such election. The like reading of the statutes afore they begin to treat of any matter shall be in all other things that have any statute appointed for them, that in often hearing and considering the words of the statutes, which they were all sworn to keep—particularly at their first entering to be a governour." The office of spokesman was considered so important that great care was exercised in seeing that he duly understood his position and responsibilities. "What he shall be sworn to do and to keep, which things be done he shall take the oath appointed for that office before he presumes to do anything belonging thereto—afterwards learn fully what his duty is to do." The fence, however, which the good Bishop was so careful in putting up, and forming, preparing it for any storm, posterity has seen broken down.

CHAPTER IX.

The "Middle Brook" like a silvery stream did flow
And "Winter Hill" was clothed in crystal snow,
When "Gorsey Brow" in tempting yellow waved.
And men for other beauties never craved.
An Eden, then, was hid within thy bowers
And Nature's gems, thy Native flowers.

THERE was a peculiar care exercised in the nomination and appointment of Governors of the school. "None shall be chosen a Governour under the full age of 24 years. The father and son shall not be Governours both at once ; nor two brethren ; nor gentlemen more than three ; nor more than two of any one town ; nor any dwelling out of the towns appointed by the Queen's letters patents to choose them of, as Rivington, Anglezargh, Foulds, Anderton, Heath Charnock, and Horwich. The Schoolmaster, Usher, and Curate shall not be chosen a governour, but it shall be well to use the assistance and advice of them and other honest neighbours as occasion shall serve. None shall be chosen a Governour also but he that is sober, wise, discreet, a favourer of God's Word, and a professor of pure religion, and is a hater of all false doctrine, Popish superstition and idolatry. Further, he that is chosen a Governour must be of honest name and behaviour —no adulterer, no fornicator, no drunkard nor gamester, no waster of his own goods, but able to live of himself. He must be chosen within one month after any room be void, or else they lose their election. The Governours must take unto them at every such election of a Governour, the Schoomaster, the Usher, and one of the discreetest men dwelling in every of the six towns aforesaid, and he that hath the most voices of these choosers shall be taken as (lawfully elected) chosen lawfully to that room ; and this election shall begin by nine o'clock in the morning, and so continue until they agree on some one. But before they give any voice, everyone, beginning at the spokesman, must take this oath following, or else he shall have no voice, and if any refuse to swear this oath they shall take another in his stead which so refuseth, and of the same town he was of, until they find one that will take the oath. And if the more part of them agree not of some one to be chosen governour before the sun be set that day, then the Master of St. John's College, in Cambridge, with two of the governours' consent, shall by their letters name and put in one to be a governour (so that he be of the towns aforesaid), whom they will, after the death of James Pilkington, now Bishop of Durham, who for his time may put in whom he will if they agree not. An Oath to be taken by all them that shall choose a governour of this school : "I, A B, take God to be my witness and judge that I, to the uttermost of my power and knowledge, and as my conscience shall bear me witness, shall not choose nor name any to be a governour of this school, at Rivington, for fear of any person, or for partial love to any part, nor for any reward given or looked for, but uprightly according to the orders already allowed by James Pilkington, Bishop of Durham, and Queen Elizabeth's grant to us made, shall name and choose such an one as I think unfeignedly to be a favourer of God's most Holy Word, and will be a furtherer of the same, forsaking all Popery and idolatry, and such a one also as is of honest life and good discretion and wealthy, and of the six towns appointed for that purpose, and also such an one as, in my opinion, will diligently save and defend the lands and goods now given or hereafter to be given or bought to this school ; and will also carefully look to the good behaviour and profit of the scholars in honesty and learning ; and will see that the schoolmaster and usher be honest in life and doctrine and diligent in teaching and doing their duties. Such a one I shall choose and name without respect of person, so help me God and His Holy Word, and as I hope to be saved by the death and bloodshed of Jesus Christ, my Lord and God."

How much like a parody would such an oath, especially if its terms were taken as an honest declaration of principles, read if now presented to the gentlemen who compose the governing board. Bishop Pilkington thought he was protecting those principles he had suffered to conserve, but like the greater proportion of bygone charities, its essence and object have been so moulded in the modern crucible, that its virtue has practically departed. " If any of the governours remove out of these six towns aforesaid, and dwell anywhere else, or be worthily put from his office for his offences, they shall choose another governour in his stead within one month next following." The duty of the governours, with the limit of their authority, is strictly defined. "The governours' charge is, first, diligently to look that the schoolmaster, usher, and scholars do their duty in teaching and learning, with honest behaviour in all times and places, and towards all persons. If the governours bear with the faults or negligence of the master, and will not remove him that doeth not his duty diligently in teaching the scholars and profitting of them, then the master of St. John's and Seniors' shall have full liberty to appoint another able man to be schoolmaster there, having such qualities as the statutes require. Likewise if they bear with the faults and negligence of the usher, and place not a better in his stead, the Bishop of Durham or Chester may place a better, which of themsoever will first do it. If the schoolmaster or usher be negligent in teaching, keep not due hours in coming to the school and continuing in it, use going to or sitting at the alehouse, be gamesters, swearers, whore hunters, quarrellers, resort not to common prayers, and the Church at appointed times, or teach anything contrary to the Holy Scriptures, or the orders appointed in this statute, or do correct their scholars too cruelly, or let them have too much liberty, the governours shall severally warn him of it, and if that amend him not they shall all, jointly together, call him or them so offending afore them, and declare his or their missbehaviour willing him or them from thenceforth to amend, and do so no more, giving him a quarter of a year's warning, to advise himself in, and try whether he will so amend. . . . The governours shall also, when any learned man cometh to the church, or near at hand, desire him to examine the schoolmaster and usher in learning and religion what standing they have. And also to try and oppose the scholars, how they profit, and such fault as the governours shall be informed to be in any of them, they shall see amended according to their discretion. One day in the first week of every quarter that school is kept, the governours shall appoint with themselves to come jointly to the school, and there learn and examine what scholars have best profitted in learning, and them that have done well they shall praise, and set him above his fellows in the same form as they found him, or else if they find it meet they shall remove him higher by the master's consent to another form." Herein we find the germ that has developed our school examinations of to-day, and though perhaps not without their incentive, and in some cases a real aid, yet they are not infallible in recording either the progress or ability of the scholars, as in many instances a mere mechanical development, and not intellectual power, or clear conception of requirements, carries the honour. Some of our most observant teachers know that oft their most brilliant boy is left behind in juxtaposition with one whom nature never meant to be his equal.

Rivington School can boast of its record of head masters, and though, perhaps, amid the rural surroundings of Rivington, the barrier which inflexible society has prescribed for the dual character of clergyman and schoolmaster is somewhat relaxed in its past history, their learning and capacity were beyond question, and the very fact of being educated at Rivington Grammar School was a potent factor in giving boys the first opportunity of entering the race of life under favourable conditions. It would be too great a task to bring before our readers the large number of local men who owe so much of their success in life's struggles to the sound and well prepared foundation laid in this school, and although its primary object is now lost, yet in the changed circumstances of its surroundings, and the better educational facilities that now prevail in the districts more immediately interested, it may perhaps be an open question if the design and object of the founder are not applied in its present condition and regulation. A few years have worked changes in other well established charities. The "Dow ut Rivington," as it was called in the vernacular of the district, is now so far circumscribed as to evoke only a limited interest. A few years ago all who loved to claim to be residents, or were by hereditary privilege connected with the villages already named, wended their way to the "Black Boy," and there received their portion of "dow." But this is now a thing of the past. One of these "Dow days" caused a converging around that ancient inn known best as "Black Lad," which now lies buried beneath the waters of the lake of the old ancients of the surrounding districts, who would almost go back to a period antecedent to

Noah's flood to prove their hereditary connection with the favoured villages rather than miss the "dow." And on such occasions no one could have returned from a peep at the human show under the shadow of the cock-crowned church without feeling that the poet was verily right in declaring that "the proper study of mankind is man." The caprices of fashion were here disregarded, and old farmers and others, whose outward appendages would suggest an affinity in point of age to the fig-leaf garments of Eden, and whose store of "spade aces" were hidden in the old oak chest with a new meal covering, would gather around the distributors and take their quota with a growling complacancy that "There'll soon be nowt to divide if yon chaps mun have their road." "Yon chaps have had their road," and, whatever may be said relative to the change, it is certainly in a direction where improvement may come if needed. But at the present it is better bestowed than in increasing the miser's hoard.

CHAPTER X.

THE scholar who had done best in these early examinations had meted out to him a reward.
"He that is found to have done best of all the school shall have authority to get his fellow's licence to play once in that term, when the govenours or master shall think metest; the meaner sort are exhorted and encouraged to ply their books, that they may likewise be exalted the next term; but those that be dullards, unthrifts, runaways, negligent, ale-house hunters, gadders in the night, truants, gamesters, dalliers with women, harlot-hunters, troublers of their fellows, pickers, brawlers, swearers, liars, tale-tellers, not given to prayer, not resorting to the church, or otherwise not profiting at their learning, these shall they correct with the rod, as the faults shall deserve, if the offender be under 16 years of age, or else with some open punishment to make ashamed as to sit in the midst of the school alone far from his fellows as long and as oft as they think fit where his fellows may finger and point (a little of the refined cruelty of the past), or keep him in the school when others play, or get rods for the correcting of his other fellows—(this would mean a ramble in Dean Wood or in some of the adjacent plantations, and perhaps to the offender would be looked upon more as a pleasure than a punishment) —or holding them up that shall be beaten, or bear the rods on high before his fellows to the church at service time, and giving him a quarter's warning to amend. But if, in his trial, he do not amend, they shall declare his behaviour to such of his friends as keep him at school, and if they will not see him corrected and amended within one quarter following, then they shall banish him from the school, that he do not infect others. But, if he be above correcting with the rod, then they shall, with the advice of the schoolmaster, appoint him to declare his faults in English (openly) first before all the school, and ask forgiveness of the same, and afterwards write a declaration in Latin against such faults as he is found guilty of. And he that is too sturdy to obey

and take these corrections shall be banished without any further bearing with him, and if any governour be absent that day without the consent of his fellows he shall pay 12 pence to the school."

We may leave for a while any further reference to the ancient regulations attached to the school, and pass on to the scheme of the Endowed School Commissioners, by which the Blackrod and Rivington Schools were reconstructed and united, and the present Elizabethan structure at the foot of Rivington Pike erected, at a cost of £9,000. The intention of the Governours was "That the school shall provide an inexpensive education to prepare boys for the Universities, the legal and medical professions, and for mercantile life." And we deem it our duty to place on record in these pages the happy choice which those entrusted with the selection have made in appointing as its first master the Rev. George Squire,M.A. (Oxon),B.A. (London), and late Exhibitioner of Balliol College, Oxford, and with whom are associated, as assistant teachers, Mr. C. A. Pauls, B.Sc., second master, with Mr. T. Williamson, Trinity College, Dublin, and Mr. J. W. Cawthorne, B.A., London. The school was opened on the "Founder's Day," 23rd January, 1882, with no flourish of trumpets, the first roll containing the names of 19 scholars and ten boarders, and amongst those present were John Longworth, Esq.,Ridgmont, Horwich (Governor), Mrs. Longworth, W. L. Longworth, Esq., W. Greenhalgh, Esq., &c. The present Governors are—Chairman, James Eckersley, Esq., Burnt House, Adlington ; Earl of Crawford and Balcarres ; Rev. W. Ritson, M.A., Vicar of Rivington ; Rev. R. C. W. Croft, M.A., Vicar of Blackrod ; Rev. C. W. N. Hutton, M.A., Rector of Standish ; J. W. Crompton, Esq.,J.P., Rivington ; Ben. Davies, Esq., J.P., Adlington Hall ; Joseph Howorth, Esq., J.P., Moor Platt, Horwich ; John Longworth, Esq., Ridgmont, Horwich ; C. E. Middleton, Esq., Heath Charnock ; E. Pilkington, Esq., Clifton House, near Manchester ; H. Rawcliffe, Esq., J.P., Gillibrand Hall, Chorley ; R. O. Spencer, Esq., Belmont, Bolton ; John Unsworth, Esq., Barker-de-lane House, Blackrod ; and E. Widdows, Esq., Adlington ; Clerk to the Governors, J. Kevan, Esq., Acresfield, Bolton. In every respect the governing body may be said to be a representative one, both socially and religiously, and gentlemen in whom the outside public repose the greatest confidence.

From the general statement we gather the following:—" That the religious instruction is in accordance with the teaching of the Church of England," but exceptions are made on the application of parents, the conscience clause prevailing. The subjects of secular instruction embrace the following :—English, Latin, Greek, and French; Mathematics (pure and applied), Chemistry, History, Geography, Drawing, Vocal Music, Book-keeping, and Shorthand. In physical science the upper boys are taught chemistry, a splendid chemical laboratory (apart from the main building) having been erected at considerable expense. Previous to admission, for which application must be made to the headmaster, who will supply the necessary form, a graduated examination takes place according to the age of the applicant, but always includes reading, writing, dictation, and the first four rules of arithmetic. The school has also the benefit of an annual examination by the Oxford University Delegacy, and all the upper boys are prepared for the Oxford Local Examinations, for which the school has been constituted a special centre, or for the London University Matriculation. The school is both ample and commodious, accommodation at present existing for fifty boarders, who are under the special supervision of the headmaster. These boarders have every opportunity for pursuing their studies with additional aids, and all their evening preparations are under the supervision of one of the resident masters. The fee on entrance is £1, day boys' fee £6 annually, the boarders, including washing and repairs, 45 guineas annually. The extras include instrumental music, 4 guineas, drill 6s., dancing (winter term) 1 guinea. A chemical laboratory is also provided, well fitted, and supplied with apparatus and chemicals, for which 7s. a term is charged. A novelty must not escape our attention in the shape of a joiners' shop, where boys are enabled to take lessons in handicraft under the guidance of a well qualified joiner, for which 7s. a term is charged. Full provision is made for the due recreation of the scholars, and this includes cricket and football. Under the heading "Exhibitions" we learn "That the Governours have power, under the scheme, to grant exhibitions, tenable in the school itself, either at admission, or on the report of the examiners and headmaster, to boys already in the school." Exhibitions are given as the reward of merit only. Other examinations are offered to be competed for, in the first instance, by boys educated in elementary schools of the following eight (8) townships of Rivington :— Anglezarke, Sharples-Higher-End, Heath Charnock, Anderton, Horwich, Adlington, and Blackrod. The present number of exhibitioners is twelve. There is also a "house scholarship" of the value of £20 a year, open to boys under 15. The governors have power to grant an exhibition of the value of £40 per annum, tenable for two years at some place of higher education, such exhibition to be competed for by boys who have been for two years in the school. The boys attend Rivington Church on Sunday morning, a service being held in the school in the evening. The boys, as they journey to church along Rivington Lane, coming in groups as circumstances favour, with academical caps, might be taken as members of some well-governed family ; but the numbers soon disperse this idea, and give place to a due recognition of the care and attention which their smart and genteel appearance demonstrates. We here give the head-master's ninth report, together with the report of the general examiner (F. G. Brabant, M.A.) :—" My lords and gentlemen,—In presenting to you my ninth annual report, I am glad to be able to state that the quality of our work during the past year has been fully maintained. The following successes have been gained during the past year—two Oxford local seniors, one in second class honours, with distinction in Latin and mathematics ; three Oxford local juniors, of whom three obtained second class honours ; and two third class honours ; and one obtained distinction in divinity, being ninth in England. One passed the Intermediate B.A. Examination of London University. The school has been examined for the fifth time by the Oxford Delagacy, and the reports of the examiners have been received, and are, on the whole, very satisfactory. The following boys are recommended for foundation scholarships in order of merit :—(Boys already holding scholarships) 1 Hargreaves (ii), 2 Buckley, 3 Unsworth, 4 Ardern (i), 5 Hough, 6 Shawcross, 7 Dixon (ii). (Boys already holding scholarships and boys in the school)—8 Slater, 9 Owen, 10 Hargreaves (ii), 11 Burgess, 12 Harper (from Adlington National School), and as vacancies occur during the year the following, in order of merit :— Booth, Ardern, Schofield, Gerrard, Lee." The report of the Special Examiner was of the most flattering description, as was that of H. G. Madan, M.A., Fellow of Queen's College, Oxford, in respect of the chemistry section. Ere we refer further to the work of this well-appreciated school we may remark *en passant* that undoubtedly the position of headmaster of the ancient Grammar School of Rivington was not always a lucrative one, and was not capable, apart from other external aid, of supporting its chief master, for in 1782 we find that the Rev. John Norcross, Head Master of Rivington Grammar School, was also curate of Horwich, and it is only by bearing in mind this dual character that some of the references made to him in the old prints can be understood, as "November 30th, 1784, Mr. Ralph Rothwell, of Brownlow Fold, Bolton, was married on Thursday to Miss Norcross, daughter of the Rev. Mr. Norcross, of Rivington." His death is thus referred to :—" July 1st, 1783. On Sunday last died the Rev. Mr. Norcross, Master of the Free Grammar School at Rivington, and curate of Horwich Church." A tombstone in Horwich churchyard, after referring to Margaret, his wife, thus records :—" The remains of the Rev. John Norcross, husband of the above, and curate of this chapel, whose preaching and worthy conduct in the station which he filled entitled him to the esteem of his congregation. He died on the 21st of June, in the year of our Lord 1788, and in the 60th year of his age." The following is an abstract of his will :— " In the name of God, amen. I, John Norcross, of Rivington, in the Parish of Bolton, and County of Lancaster, Clerk, being, through the mercy of God, sound of body, &c., do this 9th day of May, 1787, make this my last will and testament. First, I will that all my debts, funeral expenses, &c., be paid. That the Vicar of Dean and the Six Governors of Rivington School be desired to attend my funeral, and but few others, if any wishing, that as little expense may be laid upon it as possible in the mourning, and that my body be laid in the same grave with my first wife at Horwich Chapel. After that I order that my present wife—Janet—receive from my executors securities as shall please her for the sum of £475, which I had with her, and which is now placed out in my name; and also for her kind, tender, and faithful care of me and my children, the further sum of ten guineas, and five guineas more for mourning, and that she has the liberty to take all the goods which belonged to her at my marriage with her. Next, it is my will that the messuage in Withnell, with appurtenances, all my personalty, cattle, household goods or furniture, books, ready money, &c., be equally divided between my five children—Elizabeth, John, Thomas, Alice, and Margaret. And if Alice and Margaret should not be of age at the time of my decease, it is my desire that the interest of their respective shares be paid to them by my executors till they come to the age of 21 years, and then the principal be immediately paid to them. . . . In witness whereof I have herewith subscribed my name and set my seal this 9th May, 1787. Signed, sealed, published, and declared in the presence of us, William Pilkington, John Hampson, Ralph Green." The will was proved at Chester, on the 29th Dec., 1788.

CHAPTER XI.

WE place on record the report of the General Examiner for the past season, as perhaps, in juxtaposition with future reports, it will possess more than ordinary interest in determining the progress or otherwise of this highly important educational institution. "To the Governors of the Rivington and Blackrod Grammar School. My Lord and Gentlemen, I have the honour once more to lay before you the results of the examination at Rivington and Blackrod Grammar School. I have examined the papers of twelve (12) junior candidates, comprising, as I understand, the fifth form, and have taken the lower form *viva voce*. I commence with the work of the junior candidates in order. Religious knowledge: Three (3) papers were sent in, at least two of which—the Old Testament and the Acts—the results were eminently satisfactory. The third paper, on St. Mark, was not quite so well done. In the Old Testament paper, nine boys out of (12) twelve obtained over half marks. The 'Acts' were still better known, eleven (11) boys obtaining over half marks, and the leading papers showing very minute knowledge. These results quite counterbalanced a little weakness in the Gospel paper. Dixon has done very well in all three (3) papers, and Stevens also deserves mention for his Old Testament, and Gorst and Hargreaves for their 'Acts' papers. English subjects: In the English grammar paper, eight (8) boys of the twelve (12) may be considered to have done satisfactorily. The parsing is up to the mark, and the essays are, as a rule, creditable. Gorst and Dixon deserve much credit for their all round work on this paper. Hargreaves also has done well, four (4) more fairly well, while three (3) others have failed. . . . . . The Geography is quite satisfactory, the results being better than those of the History, just as they were last year. Dixon and Gorst have shown up capital papers. Of the rest, two more are above half marks, five (5) between 50 and 40 per cent., and the remaining three (3) between 40 and 30 per cent. The map was well done pretty generally by the form. In the Shakespeare paper Dixon again leads with a capital paper, showing an accurate knowledge of his author. Schofield and three (3) others have also done well. Of the rest, three (3) papers are fair, and four (4) weak. Generally speaking, the English subjects are quite satisfactory. Latin : This subject was offered by eight (8) of the junior candidates. Of these, one (Dixon) offered Virgil, but knew it only fairly well. The remainder offered Cæsar. Two (2) Leigh and Hargreaves, translated well, the rest not particularly well. The whole form, however, have done well in the unseen translation, a highly satisfactory feature. Dixon, in fact, has translated it quite correctly. He has also done a very good piece of prose. Three (3) others reach a fair level in prose. In grammar, Hargreaves has done very well, and four boys out of the eight (8) have done creditably. French : Nine (9) boys offered this subject. Two (2) of them, Dixon and Hargreaves, have done very well all round, the former conspicuously so, especially in unseen translation. Mathematics : The examiner speaks very highly of the work done under this head, the average being 81 per cent. In other respects the examiners speak very highly of the position and educational progress of the school. In the Oxford local successes we have in the Senior branch the following :—E. H. Schofield passed in religious knowledge, English, Latin, French, mathematics, 2nd class honours, with distinctions in Latin and mathematics. D. Dickinson passed in religious knowledge, Latin, and mathematics. In the junior branch W. G. Thorton passed in religious knowledge, English, Latin, Greek, French, mathematics, drawing, 2nd class honours with distinction in divinity (9th in England). G. N. Shawcross passed in religious knowledge, English, Latin, French, mathematics, chemistry, drawing, 2nd class honours. W. Dixon in religious knowledge, English, Latin, French, mathematics, drawing, 2nd class honours. T. Y. Fowler passed in religious knowledge, English, Latin, French, mathematics, chemistry, drawing, 3rd class honours. W. C. Varley in religious knowledge, English, French, mathematics, chemistry, drawing, 3rd class Honours." In addition we have the names of H. S. Gorst, G. B. Hargreaves, and J. M. B. Stubbs.

The Charter of Foundation is both explicit and instructive, and is as follows :—" Elizabeth, by the grace of God Queen of England, France, and Ireland, Defender of the Faith, &c., to all men to whom these, our present letters shall come, sends greeting: Be it known to you that upon the humble suit made to us by the Reverend Father in God, and our well-beloved James, Bishop of Durham, for our faithful liege people, inhabiting the village or hamlet of Rovington, otherwise called Rivington, within the parish of Bolton-in-the-Moors, in our County of Lancaster, and within the Diocese of Chester, for a Grammar School, there to be erected and established for ever, for a continual bringing up, teaching, and learning of children and youth of the village or hamlet of Rovington or Rivington; and also of other villages and hamlets near, adjoining the same, and of other our faithful and liege people whosoever they be, to be taught, instructed, and learned thereof, of our special grace, and sure knowledge and mere motion, we will grant, and ordain for us our heirs and successors, that hereafter there be and shall be one Grammar School in the aforesaid village or hamlet of Rovington *alias* Rivington, which shall be called 'The Free Grammar School of Queen Elizabeth,' for the bringing up, teaching, and instructing of children and youth in grammar and other good learning, to continue for ever. And we, by these presents, do erect, ordain, create, found, and establish the school of one master or teacher, and one usher, or under teacher, for ever to continue. And that our aforesaid purpose may have and take the better effect, and that the lands, tenements, rents, revenues, and other things to be granted, assigned, and appointed to the maintenance of the aforesaid school hereafter may be the better governed for sure continuance of the said school, we will ordain, and for us, our heirs and successors, do grant by these presents that hereafter there be, and shall be for ever, within the village or hamlet of Rovington, *alias* Rivington, or within the villages or hamlets next adjoining, six of the discreetest and honestest men dwelling in the said villages and hamlets for the time being, which shall be called Governours of the possessions, revenues, and goods of the Free Grammar School, that is called, and to be called the Free Grammar School of Queen Elizabeth in Rovington, *alias* Rivington, in the County of Lancaster. And, therefore, know ye, that we have assigned, chosen, nominated, and appointed for us, our heirs and successors, and do appoint our well-beloved Thomas A. Shaw, Esq., George Pilkington, Esq., Thomas Shaw, gentleman, Richard Rivington, John Green, and Ralph Whittle, for to be, and shall be the first Governours of the possessions, revenues, and goods, of the said Free Grammar School of Queen Elizabeth in Rovington, *alias* Rivington, in the County of Lancaster, well and truly to execute and occupy the said office from the day of the date of these presents, for and during their lives, so that they use themselves well and faithfully towards the said schools. And that the said Governours in deed, fact, and name, hereafter be and shall be one body corporate and politick of themselves for ever, incorporated and created by the name of Governours, of the possessions, revenues, and goods of the Free Grammar School of Queen Elizabeth, in Rovington, *alias* Rivington, in the county of Lancaster. And we do incorporate them by these presents to be Governours of the possessions, revenues, and goods of the Free Grammar School of Queen Elizabeth in Rovington *alias* Rivington in the said County of Lancaster, and we do create, erect, ordain, make, appoint, and establish them by these presents really and fully to be a body corporate and politick by the same to continue for evermore. And, furthermore, we will, and by these presents we ordain for us, our heirs, and successors, that the said Governours of the possessions, revenues, and goods of the Free Grammar School of Queen Elizabeth in Rovington *alias* Rivington, in the County of Lancaster, may have and shall have a continual succession ; and by the said name be and shall be able persons, and by the law capable to get and receive to them and their successors, being Governours of the possessions, revenues, and goods of the same Free Grammar School, manors, lands, tenements, tithes, possessions, revenues, and hereditaments, and also goods and chattels whatsoever, of us, our heirs, and successors, or of any other person or persons whatsoever. And also we ordain, grant, and decree by these presents, for us, our heirs, and successors, that so often, and whensoever it happeneth anyone or more of the aforesaid six Governours for the time being, or any other that shall be hereafter, for to die, or otherwise, were to dwell out of the town or hamlet of Rovington *alias* Rivington, and other the towns and hamlets next adjoining, or with their family to depart thence, or for their demerits and offences to be removed from the said office, that then and so often it may well, and shall be lawful to all the other aforesaid Governours then living and dwelling with their families within the said village or hamlet of Rovington *alias* Rivington and other villages and hamlets next adjoining, to choose and take unto them other eight (8) of the wisest, discreetest, and best learned men inhabiting the towns aforesaid, which being joined with the aforesaid Governours and with schoolmaster of the school aforesaid, shall choose and nominate one other meet person of the inhabitants of the village or hamlet of Rovington or Rivington, and other villages and hamlets next thereto adjoining, into the place or places of him or them so dead, deceased, or so with their families departed as is aforesaid, or of him or them that is removed from his or their office, who shall succeed and follow in the said office of Governours, and he to be considered as chosen, and be chosen, whom they all or the greatest part of them aforesaid judge and think meet to be chosen, and thus to do as often as it shall chance any room to be void. Furthermore, we will that this election be made within one month next following the vacation of any of the said Governours, and to be ended on the same day on which it is begun. And if the said election be not made in form aforesaid, then shall he be taken as chosen and be chosen only whom James, now Bishop of Durham, shall think meet to be chosen, and after his death he whom the Master of the College of St. John the Evangelist, in the University of Cambridge, with the consent of two of the Governours aforesaid, shall name shall be taken and received for a Governour, so that he, the said Master, shall appoint shall dwell within the aforesaid towns. And furthermore, we will, and for us, our heirs, and successors, grant by these presents to the aforesaid Governours and their successors, that they for ever and hereafter may have a common seal to serve for their cause and business and their successors, whatsoever are to be done. And that the said Governonrs and their successors shall and may, by the name of the aforesaid Governours of the possessions, revenues, and goods of the Free Grammar School of Queen Elizabeth in Rovington *alias* Rivington, in the County of Lancaster, may plead and be impleaded, defend and be defended, answer, and be answered in all manner of courts and places, and before any kind of judge or judges, and in what causes, actions, business, suits, complaints, pleas, and demands, of what kind, nature, or condition soever they be, or for any offences, transgressions, things, causes, or matters, by any person or persons made or done, or to be made or done by any person or persons in or upon the premises, or any parcel thereof, or touching or concerning anything specified in these presents, after the manner and form as other liege people of this our realm of England, being able persons and in law capable may plead, and be impleaded, answer and be answered, defend and be deended."

CHAPTER XII.

DOUBTLESS more in the future than in the past will the position, the government, the conditions, and the regulations that surround this school be scanned, their legality and adaptability, and their accordance with the wishes, intentions, and object of the great founder, will be more extensively criticised, and the great question evolved and forced on the interested public mind will be, how far, or how little, have the expressed intentions of the good Bishop been carried, and to what extent have the poor of the townships interested been robbed of their birthright? It is, therefore, important that such aids to judgment should be placed in the hands of the public as will enable them to form an intelligent conception of the issues. The scheme for the conjoining and working of the two endowed schools, Blackrod and Rivington, it is well to fully comprehend, hence we refer in greater detail to the scheme as submitted to the Committee of Council on Education, by the Endowed Schools Commission for the management of the "Free Grammar School of Queen Elizabeth at Rivington."

"The governing body is to consist of sixteen persons, two to be called nominated, ten representative, and four co-optative. One of the first named governours is nominated by the masters and seniors of St. John's College, Cambridge, one by the justices of the peace, in the petty sessional division within which the school is situate, and the representative as previously stated, by the townships interested, the first co-optative governours being, the Earl of Crawford, the Rev. T. Sutcliffe, Rivington, Mr. H. Rawcliffe, Haigh, and Mr. Andrew Smith, Heath Charnock. Religious opinions, or attendances, or non-attendance at any particular form of religious worship is not to affect the qualification of any person for being a governour under the scheme. The governours are to hold meetings as often as is found necessary for the management of the trust, and at least twice in each year. Any two can call a special meeting at any time, for any purpose. Abstracts of the

governours' accounts are to be published annually in
two of the local papers. As soon as practicable after
the date of the scheme the governours are to provide
for the Grammar School, buildings suitable for 110
scholars, or thereabouts, including at least fifty
boarders, with a convenient residence for the headmaster, and so arranged as to admit of convenient
extension. For these purposes the governours are to
raise and spend a sum not exceeding £5,000, unless
with consent of the Charity Commissioners. The
school is to be a day and boarding school, and no
person is to be disqualified from being a master in
it by reason of his not being, or not intending to be,
in holy orders. The headmaster is to be elected by
the governours, and he is to be a member of the
Church of England, and a graduate within some
British University. From the date of the scheme
the Rev. Septimus Tebay, the present headmaster of
the school, is to cease being master under the
trust and the governours are to pay him £400. If
Mr. Thomas Wilding, the second master, is dismissed by the governours, except for such a cause as
before the passing of the scheme they would have
been justified in doing, the governours are to pay
him £40 a year for life. Mr. Henry Francis Maltby,
present headmaster of Blackrod Grammar School,
is to continue in office as the first headmaster
until the governours think fit to make some other
arrangement. The headmaster is to give his personal attendance to the duties of the school, and
during his tenure of office he is not to accept any
benefice having the cure of souls, or any other office
which may interfere with the proper performance
of his duties as headmaster. The fixed stipend of
the master is to be £150 per annum, and
he is also allowed to receive 'head money,' calculated upon a scale to be agreed upon between him and
the governours at the rate of not less than £2 nor
more than £5 for each boy in the school. He can
also receive not less than £1 nor more than £2 a
year for each boarder. The entrance fee for boys
is to be not more than £1, and the tuition fee not
less than £3 nor more than £6 a year. The payment
of boarders is not to exceed £35 a year each. All
payments for entrance, or tuition, or for boarding
to be made in advance. No boy will be admitted
in the school under the age of eight years,
and none admitted after attaining 16 years. Any

parent or guardian of a day scholar will be at liberty to claim exemption of such scholar from attending prayer or religious worship, or from any lessons on a religious subject. The governours are to make proper regulations for the religious instruction to be given in the school, which is to be in accordance with the doctrines of the Church of England. An examination of the scholars is to be made once a year by examiners appointed for that purpose, the result of the examination to be reported to the governours, who are in turn to report the same to the head master. The governours are to apply a sum not exceeding £100 a year in providing exhibitions tenable at the school, to be granted to boys who have for two years previous to the granting of the exhibitors been educated at the public elementary schools in the eight townships or places before referred to. Each of the exhibitions is not to ex-exceed the yearly value of £10, and are to be given as the reward of merit on the result of examination for admission. Power is granted to the governors by way of further exhibitions tenable at the school, to grant exemptions from payment of tuition fees for such period, and upon such conditions as they may think fit. Boys so exempted are to be called and ranked as foundation scholars, but not more than one in twenty are to be so wholly or partly exempt. In cases of special merit the governours can grant out of the trust fund the whole or any portion of the charge of boarding, or can confer pecuniary emoluments in other ways. Each year the governours are to provide an exhibition or exhibitions of a yearly value not exceeding £40, and tenable for three years, at other places of higher education, and to be awarded by open competition among boys who have been educated at the school for two years previous to the grant of the exhibition. A yearly sum of not less than £200 is to be applied by the governours in promoting the education of girls born and living in the eight places before mentioned. For this purpose a supplementary scheme can be made by the Endowed School Commissionors, or, after their powers of making schemes has ceased, by the Charity Commissioners. Until such a scheme takes effect the governours are to apply the £200 in providing exhibitions, each of the annual value of £25, and tenable for two years at any boarding school for girls, or institution for training teachers ; such exhibitions to be awarded by competition among girls not less than fourteen and not more than eighteen years of age. Instead of applying the £200 in the manner above prescribed, the governours have power to accumulate the same, or any part of it, to provide a fund for the building of a school for girls, and when that fund amounts to £1,000 they are to apply to the proper tribunal for a scheme to establish such school. The rate of tuition fees is to be determined from time to time by the governours, but no such fee is to exceed ninepence per week. From the date of the scheme, the sites and buildings hitherto occupied for the purpose of the Blackrod Grammar School, including the master's house, are to be severed from the trust, and are to belong to the township of Blackrod, to be applied for educational purposes in the township. As soon as the funds admit, the governours are to place the sum of £1,000 consols to a separate account, the income from which is to be applied in repairs and improvements of the Grammar School when such are required. Until the repairs and improvements fund is provided, the sum of £30 is yearly to be applied to the purposes of the fund, but any surplus is to be laid by. The governours have power to form a pension or superannuation fund, the main principles being that the head master and the trust fund shall each contribute annually, for a period of twenty years, such sums as may be fixed upon, the contributions to accumulate at compound interest, and in case the head master serves his office twenty years he will be entitled, on his retirement, to the whole of the fund. Should he retire earlier on account of permanent disability from illness, he will also be entitled to the whole of the fund, and in all other cases, on ceasing to be master, he will be entitled to receive the whole of his contributions. Additional donations or endowments may be received by the governours for the general purposes of the trust, or for any special objects, the whole scheme to date from the day on which her Majesty, by order in Council, approves of it.'

The amalgamation scheme, as proposed, and as now adopted, did not meet with general approval. In one of the local newspapers, the warning sound was given in the following letter :—"Blackrod and Rivington Schools' Amalgamation Scheme. The general public is little aware of the tendency of modern legislation in the matter of endowments to benefit the *wealthier class* at the expense of the *poor.* Solomon truly says : 'The destruction of the poor is their poverty.' We have a striking instance of this in the way the Endowed Schools Commission propose to apply the funds of Rivington and Blackrod Schools ; to establish a middle class boarding and day school for boys only, which will be too far away from the homes of those residing in Sharples, Belmont, Blackrod, White Coppice, &c. There are eight townships interested in the endowments of Rivington School, Blackrod School, and Shaw's Charity, which amount to £1,250 a year. . . . Some time ago the representatives of the interested townships met, and the decision was to have several schools built in convenient localities, and to have a schoolmaster to each school. This suggestion was approved by the trustees of Rivington School and Shaw's Charity, representing an income of £950 per annum. The scheme was duly forwarded, but the Commissioners threw out the suggestion of 'boarding,' notwithstanding the fact that the position of those whom the endowments were intended to benefit would preclude them sending their children to a 'Boarding School.'" The fact that the endowments were given for the benefit of the poor of the district seemed to carry no weight with those in authority, and on the 28th of October, 1873, those for whom they were intended were virtually excluded from benefit. The scheme of the Commissioners introduced a School for Girls, but this has not been carried out."

CHAPTER XIII.

IN the south portion of the graveyard at Horwich may be seen a modest looking grave, surrounded and guarded by iron uprights, differing little to ordinary observers from many others that surround it. But if the eye wanders to a view of the monumental stone, the inscription thereon, with the stone carving at the head, the following may be read :—Crest and motto, "*Verite Sans Peur.* In memory of the Hon. Hugh, 15th Baron Willoughby, of Parnham, who resided at Shaw Place (Rivington) in this county, and who died on the 21st of January, 1765, at his house in London. Unmarried, aged 54 years." A kind of traditionary account of the time the funeral cortege was on its way, and the incidents that attended the long journey, was in the near past a subject matter of conversation with many of the old village worthies. About and surrounding this nobleman there was every inducement to foster his memory, and preserve his historic connection with Horwich. In the old parish register, at Horwich, under the date of February 9th, 1765, we have the following entry :—"The remains of the Right Honourable Hugh, Lord Willoughby, of Parnham, F.R.S., and President of the Antiquarians, London, were interred under the chancel of the chapel." Within a comparatively recent period, the inhabitants of Horwich, in the immediate vicinity of the church, had their equanimity disturbed by a rumour that the sacred precincts of God's acre had been invaded, that sacrilegeous hands were disturbing the ashes of the dead ; and in the days when stories of body snatching were not uncommon, we need not say that a slight shock was given to the village serenity. Now, however, it leaked out that the men at work were not "body snatchers," but the agents of those who wished to mark a spot where one so distinguished awaited the "Trumpet's sound." Here we enter further into the history of this grand, ancient family. We will copy for the benefit of our readers, the peculiarly shaped slab that is so conspicuous an object in the beautiful rural chapel at Rivington—an epitaph that, however much it may be regarded as incompatible with the honoured associations it records, nevertheless will prove a valuable adjunct to any future research into the past history of so historic a family. Standing a prominent object in the chapel, and recording the hereditary dignities of so noble a local family, its modesty of design, and inartistic finish, would scarcely prepare the reader for the information the pyramidal epitaph records. A little colouring is given by the adornment which a number of small shields, blazoned with armorial ensigns of the family alliances, set forth. The record is as follows: "In memory of Thomas, eleventh Lord Willoughby, of Parnham, Suffolk, of Horwich, Adlington, and Shaw Place, in this county, who died February 20th, 1691, aged 89. Also of Eleanor, Lady Willoughby, who died in 1665, aged 67. And Hugh, their eldest son, twelfth Lord Willoughby, who died in June, 1712, aged 75. Also of Anne, his lordship's first wife, who died 1690, aged 52. Likewise the Lady Honora, his second wife, eldest daughter of Lord Leigh, of Stoneleigh, and relict of Sir William Egerton, of Worsley, Knight of the Bath, second son of John Earl of Bridgewater and. his Countess, Elizabeth, daughter of his Grace the Duke of Newcastle. She died in 1750, aged 77. A truly congenial pair, fondly attached to rural scenes and retirement, and endeared to all around them by the urbanity, benevolence, and purity of their lives evinced at their favourite retreat, Worsley Hall, Lord Willoughby, in pursuits like the Noble Earl, himself a spirited agriculturist, affording employment to vast numbers on that fine domain—a dower possessed in right of her ladyship's first espousal—had iss e thereby John and Honora Egerton. Also in memory of Edward, the 13th Lord, who died unmarried in Flanders, valiantly fighting under the renowned Duke of Marlborough, in April, 1713, aged 37 years. Also of Charles, his brother, the 14th Lord, who died June 12th, 1715, aged 34, sons of the Honourable Francis. Also Hester, Lady Willoughby, his wife, who died in 1758, aged 73 years, youngest daughter of Henry Davenport, of Darcy Lever, a surviving branch of the ancient family of the Davenports, of Davenport, in the County of Chester, and eventually heiress to her brother and sister. An eminently distinguished family amongst the Dissenters at that period. Educated in the adjoining township under their relative, Oliver Heywood

M.A., the father of the Nonconformist Divines, and a native of Little Lever. Lastly in memory of the Right Honourable Hugh, their only son, and 15th Baron Willoughby, of Parnham, who expired at his house in London, unmarried, January 17th, 1765, aged 51. Interred by his Lordship's expressed desire in the family vault of his ancestors within Horwich Church, February 9th, and had a befitting funeral for so exalted a character and peer of the realm, the nobility, officers of state, patrons and directors of the various institutions joining the solemn cavalcade through the City to St. Alban's, on its route to Lancashire, which journey occupied nigh three weeks; in whom, too, the male line of the branch became extinct. A constant attender and supporter, with his revered and early-widowed and exemplary mother, of this Chapel, and to which he bequeathed the sum of £100. Here, as the Son, the Brother, the Friend, above all, as the Christian his name is perpetuated. An elegant and accomplished scholar, who, after enjoying the advantage of foreign travel for some years, returned to England filled with a patriotic devotion for his native country. Open, kind-hearted, and magnanimous, he commenced his onerous Parliamentary duties, and soon gave evidence of that legislative talent which afterwards shone forth with so much splendour, conferring upon him, by being unanimously chosen Chairman of the Committees of the House of Peers, an official reward, and the lasting esteem of his most gracious Sovereigns George II. and III. to the close of a transcendentally brilliant political career. With his universally acknowledged refinement of taste, enriched abroad, and extensively cultivated at home, and his judicious bestowal of patronage exercised in the promotion of literature, science, and the arts in whatever walk his comprehensive mind discerned genius or oppressed worth, his fostering hand brought forth the 'flower born to blush unseen,' which, in speedy requital for such true greatness of soul, obtained for him the additional very high appointments, viz., President of the Society of Antiquaries, and Vice-President of the Royal Society, succeeding the learned Martin Ffoulkes, Esq., Vice-President of the Society for the Encouragement of the Fine Arts, a Trustee of the British Museum, and one of the Commissioners of Longitude. A noble man, who adorned the title derived from his forefathers by his own social and domestic virtues, leaving a grateful nation to deplore his unexpected removal from this sublunary state, and two sisters, his co-heiresses at law, the Hon. Helena, wife of Baxter Roscoe, Esq., and the Hon. Elizabeth, the wife of John Shaw, Esq. As a tribute of affectionate regard due to so lamented a servant, philanthropist, and relative, this monument is erected by his grandnephews and nieces :—

> 'Friends we have had—the years flew by,
> How many have they borne away?
> Man, like the hours, is borne to die,
> The last year's hours, oh, where are they?
> Catch then, O catch the transcient hour,
> Improve each moment as it flies;
> So teach us, in our solemn hour,
> That we ourselves are dying flowers.
> He dies, alas! how soon he dies,
> Yet all these flowers now lost by death
> In other worlds shall brightly bloom,
> Spring with fresh life, immortal breath,
> And burst the confines of the tomb."

The connection of the Willoughbys with this part of Lancashire had, as we have before stated, its beginning in the marriage of Thomas Willoughby with Eleanor, daughter of Hugh Whittal (Whittle), of Horwich, who was a stern old Puritan, and who is often referred to by some of the Puritan writers. The Willoughbys were of a family ancient and illustrious in lineage, the patronymic being derived from the Willoughby Manor in Lincolnshire, and where they had been seated almost from the time of the Conquest. The sign of the village Inn, the "Black Lad," is said to be derived from an exploit that occurred in Palestine, when Sir William, having joined the "Army of the Cross" under young Prince Edward, fought against the Turks. In almost every page in the history of the stirring events of a bye-gone period the name of Willoughby, either from the direct parent, stock, or collaterally, is to be found. Few of our readers but will know that now ancient looking farm stead, known by the name of Shaw Place, with its quaint surroundings, its long range of out-buildings, and with a gable upon which a tablet is inserted, bearing the inscription "W.H.H., 1705," and which doubtless refers to Hugh, the twelfth Lord Willoughby and Lady Honora, his wife, and no doubt erected in the earlier part of Queen Anne's reign. Inside the house are many reminiscences of its lordly owner, but the hand of time and the repeated alterations have destroyed some of the more valuable relics. Even the carved stone work has not been unmolested, and only a remnant is left to tell of its past history.

CHAPTER XIV.

"The brave Lord Willoughby,
Of courage fierce and fell,
Who would not give one inch of way
For all the devils in hell."

IN "The Genealogist," edited by George W. Marshall, LL.D., F.S.A., for January, 1880, under the heading of "The Barony of Willoughby of Parham. Is it Extinct?" we have the following able article, which, for the benefit of our readers, and a due acknowledgment to its able writer, we take the liberty of copying, feeling assured that the utmost confidence may be placed in it. The heading is unique, and refers to the many futile efforts that have been made to breathe life into the dry bones of this ancient and historic peerage. "On the 16th February, 1547 (1st Edward VI.) Sir William Willoughby of Parham, Co. Suffolk), the representative of the ancient family of Willoughby, of Willoughby, was raised to the peerage by letters patent under the title of Baron Willoughby of Parham, with the usual remainder to the heirs male of his body. In this dignity he was succeeded by his only son Charles, second baron, who, by his wife, the Lady Margaret Clinton, third daughter of Edward, first Earl of Lincoln, had (with other issue who died s.p.), three sons, viz. (1) William, his heir, who died in his father's lifetime, leaving issue (2) Ambrose, (3) Thomas. Upon the decease of Charles, second Lord Willoughby of Parham, in 1603, the peerage descended to his grandson William, third baron (eldest son of the Hon. William Willoughby, who died *vitra patris*), and in his descendants the dignity continued until Charles, tenth baron, who died 9th December, 1679, without issue; devising his estate to his niece Elizabeth, the wife of the Hon. James Bertie, ancestor of the present Earl of Abingdon. With the tenth lord the whole of the male descendants of the Hon. William Willoughby, eldest son of Charles, second baron, failed. The barony should now by right have devolved upon the heir of Sir Ambrose Willoughby, the second son of the second lord. Sir Ambrose married Susan, daughter of Richard Brookes, of Matson, co., Gloucester, Esq., and by her had an only son, Edward Willoughby, who, by his wife Rebecca, daughter of Henry Draper, Esq., left two sons, Henry and Richard. The elder of these should have inherited at the decease of the tenth lord; but having with his family emigrated to Virginia, his existence was lost sight of, and as no claim to the title was put forth by this branch of the family, it was presumed that the descendants of Sir Ambrose Willoughby had become extinct. Under these circumstances, Thomas Willoughby, son and heir of Sir Thomas, the third surviving son of the second baron, asserted his claim to the dignity, and, meeting with no opposition, the claim was allowed. On the 19th May, 1685, Thomas Willoughby was summoned to Parliament by writ, addressed 'Thomas Willoughby de Parham Chir. (Dugdale 'Summonses to Parliament') and took his seat in the House of Peers accordingly, ostensibly as the eleventh baron under the patent of 1547. In his line the dignity continued for eighty years, until on the decease of Hugh, fifteenth baron, 21st January, 1765 (referred to in last chapter) without issue, the entire male descent of the 11th baron, and of his father, the Hon. Sir Thomas, terminated. In the meantime the descendant of Sir Ambrose, becoming acquainted with his right to the peerage, came back from America, proved his pedigree, and asserted his claim, creating thus, says Sir Bernard Burke (Extinct Peerage, ed. 1866) a condition of things most unprecedented in the annals of the peerage. He, the true lord, was excluded from his true rights as a peer, while his cousin, the false lord, sat and voted. The extraordinary state of things was, however, ended by the death of Hugh, fifteenth baron, in 1765. Henry Willoughby, the grandson and heir of Henry Willoughby, who had emigrated to America, then put in his claim to the peerage. After a solemn hearing before the House of Lords the title was adjudged to him in 1767 by the following memorable decision:—'That he had a right to the title, dignity, and peerage of Willoughby, of Parham, which was enjoyed from the year 1680 to 1765 by the male line (now extinct) of Sir Thomas Willoughby, youngest son of Charles, Lord Willoughby, of Parham, who were successively summoned to Parliament by descent, in virtue of letters patent, contrary to the right and truth of the case, it now appearing that Sir Ambrose Willoughby, the second son of the said Charles (and elder brother of the said Thomas), who was averred to have died without issue, left a son; and that Henry Willoughby, Esquire, the claimant, is great grandson and heir male of the said Sir William, who was created Lord Willoughby of Parham, the male line of the eldest son of Charles, Lord Willoughby of Parham, having failed in or before the year 1680 (Dormant and Extinct Baronage, by T. C. Banks, ed., 1809, vol. iii., 747). In accordance with this decision, on the 25th April, 1767, Mr. Henry Willoughby took his seat in the House of Peers as sixteenth baron. He died in 1775 without issue, and was succeeded by his brother George, seventeenth baron, at whose decease in 1779, also without issue, the whole of the male descendants of William, first baron, appear to have failed, and the barony created by letters patent in 1547 consequently became extinct. The decision of the House of Peers in 1767, so far from ending all perplexity connected with the title of Willoughby of Parham, opens up an important question as to the after descent of the dignity. The singular mistake by which the younger line was allowed the title upon the presumption that the issue male of the elder branch had failed, together with the *legal* admission of the error in the judgment of 1767, casts considerable doubt upon the *extinction of the peerage*, if indeed it does not clearly point to the contrary. In more than one instance it has been determined that wherever a Writ of Summons to Parliament is issued, under the presumption that a barony is vested in the person to whom the Writ is addressed, although it shall afterwards appear that no such Barony is vested in the person so summoned, yet such Writ of Summons and a sitting under it *creates a barony in fee* to the individual who receives it, and to the heirs of his body. (Courthope's Historic Peerage, Ed. 1857, p. xli). This doctrine was clearly established in 1736 in the claim to the Barony of Strange, and confirmed in the following year in the case of the Barony of Clifford. The judgment of the peers in 1767, by which the Barony of Willoughby was adjudged to the representative of the elder line, expressly declares that the preceding lords had, for nearly a century been summoned to Parliament contrary to the right and truth of the case. In point of fact, neither Thomas, called eleventh baron, nor his descendants were ever in legal possession of the Barony of Willoughby, created by the patent of 1547. They received Writs of Summons, and sat and voted in Parliament, but the peerage which was supposed to confer the authority for their so doing was not theirs, but properly belonged to, and, during the whole of the period in question, was actually vested in the elder line, whose right remained, although the enjoyment of the same was postponed owing to the omission to claim at the time it first accrued. The condition of things from 1685 to 1765 as to the Barony of Willoughby, of Parham, was this: The senior line of the family in which the peerage of 1547 undoubtedly was vested was excluded the enjoyment of the peerage rights, while successive generations of a younger branch sat and voted in the House as Barons Willoughby of Parham. The latter were certainly Peers of Parliament, inasmuch as they received Writs of Summons, and enjoyed the rank and privileges of barons. But as certainly they were *not* in possession of the barony under which they were supposed to sit. The question then arises—*what peerage* did they hold ? The decisions before referred to in the cases of the Baronies of Strange and Clifford, seem to leave little room for doubt upon the point. Thomas Willoughby was summoned to Parliament in 1685 under the supposition that he had inherited the Barony of Willoughby of Parham, but which after circumstances proved was at that very time vested in another person. Under such writ he sat and voted in the House, as did his descendants after him. The law in such cases is clear: 'If a commoner is summoned to Parliament, and sits under such summons, his blood is ennobled, and the title and dignity descend to his heirs.' (Cruise on Dignities, p. 202.) Thomas Willoughby when summoned was undoubtedly a commoner, inasmuch as the peerage he was supposed to hold was the property of another, consequently the Writ of Summons to him must, it is assumed, be regarded as a creation *de novo*. Immediately upon his receiving the writ, and in obedience thereto, sitting under it, he became entitled to a barony in fee, inheritable after the manner of all such baronies by his heirs general, both male and female. The circumstance that he was called Lord Willoughby, of Parham, while at the same time another person was in existence entitled to the same designation, does not in any way militate against this view. It is quite within the province of the Sovereign to summon to Parliament two persons by the same name and title, and many instances are on record where this has been done. Neither does the fact that Thomas Willoughby and his descendants were placed in the precedence of the barony of 1547 interfere with their title to the peerage. A mistake in the matter of precedence is a point that at any time can be rectified by the House (Cruise pp. 196, 197). To summarise the whole, two (2) distinct baronies of Willoughby of Parham have, it may be assumed from the foregoing premises, been called into existence, the first by letters patent to Sir William Willoughby in 1547, and which, in accordance with the terms of the patent, became extinct upon the failure of the issue male of the first lord in 1779; the second by Writ of Summons to Thomas Willoughby in 1685, which, being a barony in fee, is inheritable by his heirs general. Hugh, called Fifteenth Baron Willoughby, but, in reality, fifth baron under the writ of 1685, was the last male descendant of this line. Upon his death in 1765, unmarried, the title fell into abeyance between his two sisters and co-heir, and thus remains amongst their descendants and representatives to the present time. If the foregoing assumption as to the existence of a barony in fee be correct, and it is submitted there is strong reason for believing so, it becomes of importance to inquire as to the person or persons who would now be entitled to claim such barony. Upon this point the annexed pedigrees, compiled chiefly from information supplied by members of the family, and giving the descendants of Thomas Willoughby, who was summoned by Writ in 1685, will, I think, be of interest.

The above article is signed by Wm. Duncombe Pink, Leigh, Lancashire.

Descendants of Thomas, Baron Willoughby De Parham, summ. to Parl., 1685.

Thomas Willoughby, son and heir of Sir Thomas Willoughby, fifth son of Charles, second Baron Willoughby, of Parham, summ. to Parl. by Writ (1 James II), 19 May, 1685, as "Baron Willoughby de Parham;" died 29 Feb., 1691-2, aged 89, leaving issue by his wife Eleanor, dau. of Hugh Whittle, of Horwich, co. Lanc. (The Hugh Whittle, of Hor wich, here referred to, was of an ancient Horwich family. Whittles, Higher and Lower House,—a portion of the latter being covered with the L. and Y. Railway works—were inhabitants of note).

I. Hugh Willoughby, eldest son, who succeeded.

II. Francis Willoughby, second son, married Eleanor, dau. of Thomas Rothwell, of Haigh, co. Lanc., who was living in 1713. They had issue :—

  1. Thomas Willoughby, eldest son, born 4 Mar., 1674. Died unmarried. Buried at Horwich, 29 Sep., 1703.

  2. Edward Willoughby. ⎱ Successively 13th and
  3. Charles Willoughby. ⎰   14th Barons.

  4. Hugh, born 27th July, 1685 ; living 1693 ; died unmarried.

  1. Eleanor, born 16th May, 1669.
  2. Alice, born 6th November, 1691.
  3. Margaret, born 10th August, 1673.
  4. Hannah, born 15th October, 1679.
  5. Mary, born 17th May, 1683.
  6. Sarah, born 25th March, 1687.
  7. Rebecca, born 25th January, 1690.

III.—Jonathan Willoughby, third son, mar. 28th July, 1696 ; buried at Horwich, 5th September, 1696., s.p.

  1. Mary, marr. Samuel Greenhalgh, of Adlington, co. Lanc.
  2. Sarah.
  3. Abigail.

Hugh Willoughby, eldest son, succeeded his father as 12th (2nd ?) Baron Willoughby, 29th February, 1691-2 ; died August, 1712, s.p.s. He married twice —first, Anne, dau. of Lawrence Halliwell, of Tockholes, co. Lanc. ; secondly, Honora, dau. of Sir Thomas Leigh (son and heir-apparent of Thomas, first Lord Leigh, of Stoneleigh, co. Warwick), and widow of Sir William Egerton, of Worsley, co. Lanc.

Edward Willoughby, nephew and heir, born April 12th, 1676, succeeded as 13th (3rd) Baron Willoughby, August, 1712, and sat first in Parliament, 13th January, 1712-13 ; died 13th April, 1713, s.p. Admon. granted at Chester 6th May, 1713, to a creditor, on the renunciation of his mother and brother.

CHAPTER XV.

"CHARLES Willoughby, brother and heir, born 25th December, 1681, succeeded as 14th (4th) Baron Willoughby, April 1713, died 21 June, 1715. Will dated 12 May, proved at Chester, 6 Aug., 1715. Married Hester, daughter of Henry Davenport, of Darcy Lever, Lancashire, by whom (who married, secondly, James Walton, of Heath Charnock, Co. Lanc.) she left issue—Hugh Willoughby, son and heir, who succeeded, Helena Willoughby, married Baxter Roscoe, of Anglezark, and Elizabeth Willoughby, who married John Shaw, of Shaw Place, Rivington." From this branch sprang the Shaws, of Rivington, the male representative being Richard Shaw, of Gilsbrook, in that township, eldest son of Charles Shaw, who died in 1861. James Shaw, the second son, is General Superintendent of the L. & N.-W. Railway, at Liverpool. To those of our readers who wish more fully to trace this historic local family, I would refer to the "Genealogist," edited by George William Marshall, L.L.D., F.S.A, Jan., 1880. It is beyond our province, in the limited space at our disposal, to trace the collateral branches of this important aristocratic family. Much has already been written on the subject, and from the grand old trunk many of our local families draw their distinction, and justly pride themselves on their hereditary descent. The Lord Willoughby to whom we have more especially referred was distinguished by a broad and sympathetic view on religious matters, and a complaint was made to the Bishop of Chester, in whose diocese Horwich then was (1717) by the then Vicar of Deane (the Rev. Richard Hatton), "That the chappell at Horwich has for ye 20 years last been in the hands of ye Dissenters, thro' ye contrivance of ye late Lord Willoughby." Here we may allude to the connection of the Willoughbys with Horwich, a connection which doubtless gave "Lord's Height" its name, and the farm which includes the old Racecourse, its distinction. That the Willoughbys were extensive landowners in the townships immediately surrounding is beyond question, and that their influence and power were almost superlative is proved by the many references to them in the old records of the district. In connection with this more local aspect of our inquiry, we would refer to a letter in the *Bolton Weekly Journal*, October 2, 1878, signed M. and A. Mason, Foxholes House, descendants on the maternal side. It says 'You were quite right in saying that they (Willoughbys) were of Horwich. It was prior to Shaw Place (Rivington), the ancient residence, being at that which is now called the Old Lord's, in Horwich—being then in tenement—and adjoining their other property, Lower Knowle, Rivington. The old mansion has been taken down and a modern structure erected. A few years since there was a large stone at the top of the field called The Lord's Height, formed by the waters into the shape of a chair, called Lord Willoughby's chair, on which his lordship frequently sat when taking a survey of the country around. Lord Willoughby held a mortgage on Shaw Place, then purchased it, and afterwards it became the family seat. Four (4) of the Lords Willoughby are buried at Horwich Church. The vault was situated in the chancel under the east window in the old edifice. About the year 1831 the present church was built. (The first stone of the present church was laid May 31st, 1830, by Joseph Ridgway, Esq., J.P., D.L.) Now the vault is on the outside with a handsome tomb, on which is engraved the Willoughby coat of arms, the hatchment being on the south wall inside the church." J. B. Williams, F.S.A., London, in his "Life, Character, and Writings of the Rev. Mathew Henry," says:— "He was intimate with Lord Willoughby, 14th baron (Lord Charles), and after preaching at Chowbent it was no uncommon thing to trace him from the conventicle to his lordship's seat." In 1708 he describes him as a very grave, serious nobleman, showing him great respect, and speaking with fervour of Divine things. Lady Esther, relict of the 14th baron, died January, 1761, and was buried at Horwich. The Willoughbys possessed land in Horwich, Rivington, Heath Charnock, Blackrod, &c. Much has been said of Lord Willoughby, 15th baron, of his high position, &c. He was an eminent Christian, a man of much prayer, a humble follower of his Lord and Saviour Jesus Christ.

When absent from his other duties he was often found in the cottages of the poor. In person he was a tall, handsome-looking nobleman, with lofty brow and serious face. The last time he left Shaw Place for London on his Parliamentary duties he did not join the stage coach at Anderton, but walked through Rivington to Marklands, Horwich, and joined the coach near Moor Platt. His illness was short. One night he was taken ill, and aroused his valet, and the services of three physicians were called in, Dr. Leak, Dr. Watson, Dr. Triquet. He had great respect for Horwich as the ancient seat and burial place of his noble ancestors, and as he lay on his death bed he said to those around him " Take me to Horwich." Accordingly after three (3) weeks journey on the road he was brought in a coffin covered with crimson velvet and many handsome plates upon it, and laid in the family vault. Our paternal grandfather paid the last tribute of respect by attending his funeral."

·It will perhaps be not out of place here to introduce some extracts from the diary of Lady Willoughby, not only as giving the quaint and expressive manner of the more learned of the period, but also because of its direct and homely description of a most important epoch in English history—a period which doubtless has exercised a more potent effect on the progress, the civil, and religious liberty of the nation than any other in the annals of our history, and however much we may deplore the "holy riot," the religious caricatures which the period called forth—those days when England had no King, and religion was more of an outward sign than an invisible grace, they were the percursors of the grand liberties and great privileges which are the boast and the pride of the "Sons of Albion." To read the events of the past in the light of the 19th century is to traduce the characters of some of the noblest patriots that bled and died in "Freedom's hoary battle." Rather let us look with sorrowful eye on their mistakes, while we thank God for the blessings that hath sprung therefrom.

To quote from Lady Willoughby's diary :—" May 13, 1635, Tuesday, 'A Rose at my usual houre, six of the clock, for the first time since the Birth of my little sonne ; opened the casement, and looked forth upon the Park ; a herd of Deer pass'd bye, leaving the traces of their footsteps in the dewy grasse. The

Birds sang; and the aire was sweet with the scent of the wood-binde and the fresh birch leaves. Took down my Bible; found the Mark at the 103d Psalm, read the same, and returned Thanks to Almighty God that he had brought me safely through my late Peril and Extremity, and in His great Bountie had given me a deare little One. Pray'd Him to assist me by His Divine Grace in the right performance of my new and sacred duties; truly I am a young mother, and need Help. Sent a Message to my Lord, that if it so pleased him, I would take Breakfast with him in the Blue Parlour. At Noon walked out on the South Terrace; the two Greyhounds came leaping towards me; divers household affaires in the course of the Day; enough wearied when night came. May 19, Tuesday. Had a disturbed night, and rose late, not down till after seven; Thoughts wandering at Prayers. The Chaplain detained us after Service to know our Pleasure concerning the Christening. My Lord doth wish nothing omitted that should seem proper to signify his respect to that Religious Ordinance which admits his child into the outward and visible Church of Christ, and gives honour to his firstborn sonne. During Breakfast we gave the subject much consideration. My Husband doth not desire him to be named after himself, but rather after his Father; his Brother William therefore bearing his name, will stand Godfather. All being at last brought to a satisfactory conclusion, he went forth with the Chaplain and gave his orders accordingly therewith, I doing the same in my smaller capacity, he for whom was all this care lying unconsciously in his nurse's arms. Messenger from Wimbleton. My deare and honoured Mother writes that she doth at present intend setting forth on Monday; gave orders for the East Chamber to be prepared. The day being fine walked down to the Dairy; told Cicely to make Cheese as often as will suit, the whey being much approved by my Mother. The brindled Cow calved yesterday; Calf to be reared, as Cicely tells me the Mother is the best milker we have. Daisy grows and promises to be a fine cow; praised Cicely for the cleane and orderly state of all under her care; she is a good, clever Lasse. As I returned to the house mett my Lord, who had come to seeke me; two Strangers with him; thought as he drew near how comely was his countenance; he advanced a pace or two before the others, took my hand, and pressed it to his lips, as he turned and introduced me to Sir Arthur Hazelrigge and the Lord Brooke. Methought the latter very pleasing, of graceful carriage, and free from any courtly foppery and extravagance in his apparel. They presently renewed their conversation respecting New England. Lord Brooke and Lord Say and Sele have sent over Mr. George Fenwicke to purchase land and commence building; there is talk of Mr. John Hampden joining them. Lord Brooke discoursed at length on the admirable qualities and excellent attainments of the late Lord, his cousin, who came by a cruel death, being murdered by his servant through a jealousy he entertained that his past services were neglected. Some members of my lord's family knew him well; and did see much of him when Sir Fulke Greville; he was greatly esteemed by many, but known chiefly as the friend and lover of Sir Philip Sydney, whose early death was mourned by all England, and whose like may not again be looked upon. He left directions that their friendship should be recorded on his tomb, as may be scene in Warwick Church: *Fulke Greville, Servant to Queen Elizabeth, Councillor to King James, and Friend to Sir Philip Sydney.* July 15th, Wednesday.—Bade Alice take heed there should be good store of chamomile flowers and poppyheads, and of mint water; our poore neighbours look to us for such. John took the yarn to the weaver's, and brought back flax, spices, and sugar.—Aug. 17, Monday: Walked down to the keeper's lodge; old Bridget suffers from the rhewmatickes; bid her send to the hall for a plaister and some flannel; did my endeavours to persuade her that the same would bee of greater service than the charm given her by Dame Stitchley, though as she would not consent to leave it off, doubtlesse it will gaine all the credit should Bridget's aches and paynes seem to amend. Tydings of my deare Lord. He speaks much in his letter of a painter named Vandyck, who stands in great favour at Court. The King, the Princes, and the Princess Mary have sat to him. The ladies crowd to his painting room desirous to see themselves perpetuated by his graceful pencil."

Shaw Place, at present, is divested of much that once told of times when within its gates was all that made up "The fine old English gentleman, all of the olden time." The unique architecture has so far been disturbed as to lose its pristine aspect, its outer walls have been robbed under the mistaken idea of enriching a modern mansion, the globular stone mountings that stood upon its ancient gates are debased in the more modern surroundings of "The Street," and the vandalism that destroyed its ancient yew tree, and left its hoary trunk to be despoiled and neglected in the Public Hall Green, at Horwich, bespeak a callousness to things ancient that the future will mourn in vain. Rivington in this respect has been verily crucified. Its old paths have been torn up, its ancient landmarks removed, its rural beauties closed, and, where nature intended man to observe and worship her handiwork, he has defaced her temple, and would still deny to others a peep within those lovely groves and shaded bowers where the holiest inspiration springs, and the truest worship is fostered.

CHAPTER XVI.

THE following is a continuation of Lady Willoughby's diary :—

"1635, November 24th, Tuesday. The heavy raines of late have made much sicknesse to abound. Through mercy our family are preserved in health, and baby has cut a tooth, discovered this morning by the spoon knocking against. One Thomas Parr is dead at a wonderfull greate age, being, it is said, 150 yeares old. The Earle of Arundell had him brought to Whitehall, and the change did shortly affect his health ; no marvel, poore old man, he would have been better pleased, methinks, to have beene lett alone. 1635-6. The Hollanders have sent an Embassy and a noble present on the occasion of the Queene having another daughter ; these are rare pieces of china and paintings, one by Tytian. When at Lincoln my Lord tooke me to the Cathedral, and showed me the tomb of his late father, who died in that citie in the yeare 1617. May Day, 1637. We walked down to the village at an early houre, just in time to see the procession of the May-pole, which was adorned with ribbons and garlands. Lads and lasses were at their merry games, the Queene in her holie-day finery and crowne of floures, looking happier than the wearer of a real crown, I ween, groups of old people looking on. For a while there was a lack of young men and maidens. But a number shortly appeared as Robin Hood, Maid Marien, and methought some of the elder folks looked grave ; and at one side of the green a stern looking man, dressed in a loose coat and a high crown'd hat, with the hair cut close, had collected a good many round him, and was holding forth in a loud harsh tone. The speaker set forth the diabolical wickedness of the dance, and the vanity of such amusements. After a while the sport seeming to flag, my Lord offer'd to head a party at prison bars, and William Willoughby coming up with a sonne of Sir Robert Crane and one or two more young men, the game was sett on with great spirit. Ale and victuals came down from the Hall.

June 27th, Tuesday. At noon to-day we walked down to the sheep-shearing; the poor sheep struggle against their fate, but how quietly do they submit in the end. The lambs did keep up a contiued bleating, it is a marvel how they find out their own mothers, who come back to them so changed. On our way home two curly-headed children presented us with Posies of Gilliflowers and Cowslip tufts. Bade them go up to the Hall with them. We gave them a Silver Groat. July 19th, 1637. Wednesday. Late in the day Mr. Gage rode up. He tells us that Mr. John Hampden hath refused the late demand for Ship Money. Discontent everywhere. The proceedings in the Starre Chamber against Prynne and others have roused the whole country. Even many who tooke not part with the malcontents doe now expresse their Abhorrence of this Tyranny. My Husband will go to London straightaway. July 14th, Monday, 1637. With a heavy heart saw my deare Lord depart this forenoon. July 25th, Tuesday. To-night John Armstrong returned bearing me a kind farewell from his Master. He sayeth Mr. John Hampden's Refusal is greatly talked about. Likewise it is rumoured the Lord Say hath refused the demand for Ship Money with equal pertinatiousnesse. Armstrong stopped as he passed through Wickham at the Blacksmith's, the Headquarters of News and Country Gossip. He there met with a Packman, who says there be terrible tumults in the North. At Edenburgh the Bishop well-nigh killed. Stones and other Missiles thrown at him in the pulpit, so soon as he commenced reading the Prayer Booke, as ordered in Councill. On leaving the Church he was cast down and nearly trod to death. Some say the King is like to go to Edenburgh to settle these matters in person with the Presbytery. Augt. 5th, Thursday. Tidings of my Lord; he keeps well in health, he saith judgement in Mr. Hampden's cause is deferred till next term. Two of the Judges are on his side. 1638-9. [Date wanting.] Since Judgement hath been given against Mr. Hampden, my dear Husband hath had divers conferences with the Lords Say and Brooke respecting their leaving the country. One, Mr. Oliver Cromwell, they speak of, as much stirred by the unhappy state of affairs, and they have found him to be a man of shrewd judgment, and possessing great energy and determination. The King at Yorke, and has required the nobility and officers to take an oath that they do abhor all rebellions, and especially such as do arise out of religion. The Lords Say and Brooke refusing to take the same have been dismissed to their homes. The King proceedeth to Berwick, there to meet the Scotch deputies. Much discontent that the King calleth no Parliament. 1639-40, January 1, Wednesday. My first thoughts are due to Thee, O, Heavenly Father, who hast mercifully permitted the past yeare to close and the present to open upon us a thankful and happy family. Graciously accept my imperfect thanksgiving, and the adoration of a heart which I, with unfeigned humility anew, dedicate to Thee. By the aide of Thy Holy Spirit lead me every day I live to love Thee more worthily, and serve Thee more acceptably. May I truly repent of my manifold transgressions, my pride, my rebellious spirit, which hath too often struggled against the just appointments of Thy providence. Do Thou, O God, renew a light spiritt within me. Lord, Thou hast made mee to be a mother, oh yet, spare the sweet children Thou hast given unto me, and may I never lose sight of the duty which is entrusted to me, but so train them that they may be all gathered into Thy fold at the greate day of account, may Thy blessing rest upon them, upon my husband, and on all deare to unto us. And to Thy fatherly care, Thy wisdom, and Thy love may we trust all that concerns us in unshaken faith, and in the blessed hope of eternal life, through Jesus Christ our Lord and Saviour. Took De by the hand and went down to prayers. Me thought the chaplain's discourse savoured somewhat of pharisaical gloom and austerity; and we were, therefore, in no little perplexity when Armstrong came into the Hall after breakfast to say the domestics petition'd for a dance and Christmasse Games to-night, according to old usage. We gave our consent. The Chaplain expressed his dissatisfaction, neverthelesse the evening past merrily. A goodly assembly were gathered together of our neighbours, and to show our goodwill we looked on for a while, and my lord led off the firste dance with the Bailiff's daughter. The young men of our party followed his example, and chose out the prettiestlooking damsels, my favourite Cicely being one of them, and they went down a long country dance. Old Blind John and his Son played the viol and pipe. Games followed, bob-apple and the like. May

7th, Thursday. Newes hath reached us that the King has dissolved the Parliament though so lately mett, he being offended by the Commons passing a Resolution that the Discussion and Redresse of Grievances should preceede the Vote of Supply. They complained that the interference of the Lords was a violation of their privileges. An eloquent speech by Mr. Waller. Such a House suited not the King. 1640, May 9th. Saturday. My husband writes me word that Mr. Bellasis and Sir John Hotham are sent to the Tower—onely offence alleged, their speeches—the house of the Lord Brooke searched for papers; his study and cabinets broken open. A Convocation of Clergy hath bene held; the canons issued by them such as to throw the whole nation into a ferment. Writs of Ship-money in greater number than ever and Bullion seized, the property of merchants, and kept by them in the Tower for safety. . . . A visit to Old Betty's Cottage seldom faileth to give me such sense of her truly virtuous and pious life. She hath lost Husband and children, save one son onely, who left her years agoe; she hath been totally blind more than fifteen yeares. Wednesday, May 27. The Mayor and Sheriffe of London have been brought before the Starre Chamber for slacknesse in levying the ship money. Sep. 16, Saturday, 1640. Lord Say writes that a Petition has beene presented to the King by twelve Peers, praying him to call a Parliament, so likewise have the citizens of London. Oct. 20, Tuesday, 1640. Messenger arrived from the Mayor of Ipswich; writts are issued for the 3rd of Nov. . It is hoped Mr. Oliver Cromwell will be returned for Cambridge. My deare Husband hath again departed. Nov. 9th, Monday. The King hath opened Parliament in person. They say he looked pale and dejected. The Commons hath made choice in haste of Lenthall, a barrister, for Speaker, instead of one Gardiner, he being the King's choice. They have passed a Resolution that *Prynne, Burton*, and Dr. Bastwick should be sent for forthwith by Warrant of the House. The Table is loaded with Petitions, presented by hundreds crying out, '*No Bishops; No Starre Chamber.*' December 2, Wednesday. On the 28th the three *Puritans*, as they are called, liberated from their distant dungeons, came up to London, and were mett by 5,000 persons. Dec. 15, Tuesday. Heard to-day that the Earle of Strafford was committed to the Tower. It is say'd he urgently declined appearing in the House, but the King insisted, making him solemn assurances of safety. But he no sooner entered the House than he was put under arrest. Dec. 24, Thursday. The determined measures of the Commons fill all the people with amazement. The Archbishop of Canterbury is accused of high treason, and committed to the usher. It is sayd he hath been forced to sell his plate to raise money wherewith to pay the fine of £500. And a resolution has been passed that for bishops or other clergymen to be in the Commission of the Peace, or to have any judicial powers in the Starre Chamber, or in any Civil Courts, is a hindrance to their spiritual functions, &c. This seemeth true enough; greate neede have all parties to pray to be preserved from excesses, or being carried away by the heate of party spirit and personal resentment. The cruelty and severity exercised by Archbishop Laud in Scotland, and the Earl's tyranny and wickednesse in Ireland, have raised them enemies, who wish nothing so much as their death."

CHAPTER XVII.

"1640-1.—March 6, Saturday. On Monday [so continues Lady Willoughby's diary] the Archbishop (Laud) was removed to the Tower from Master Maxwell's house, where he hath beene allowed to remain since his commitment. From Cheapside to the Tower he was followed and railed at by the people, the which he took quitely. . . . I may here write an Inscription to the Memory of the late Mistress Hampden, which my Lord did copy from her Tomb in the Church at Great Hampden, when he was last at that place. . 'To the eternal Memory of the truly Vertuous and Pius *Elizabeth Hampden*, Wife of *John Hampden*, the tender Mother of an happy Offspring in 9 hopefull children. In her Pilgrimage the Staie and Comfort of her Neighbours, the Love and Glory of a well-ordered Family, the Delight and Happinesse of tender Parents, but a Crowne of Blessings to a Husband. In a Wife ; to all an eternal Paterne of Goodnesse, and Cause of Joye, whilst she was, in her dissolution, a Losse unvalwable to each. Yet herselfe blest, and they recompensed, in her Transition from a Tabernacle of Claye and fellowshipp with Mortalls to a celestial Mansion and Communion with *Deity*, the 20th Day of August, 1634. *John* Hampden, her sorrofull Husband, in perpetual Testimony of his conjugal Love, hath dedicated this Monument.'" . .

"Lady Day, March 25, Thursday, 1641. In the Steward's Room two or three Houres, paying out Wages and so forth, and looking over Armstrong's Bookes. The last yeare's Wool was sold, the greater part thereof to the Baize-maker at Colchester, at 24 Shillings the Tod, a better Price than hath been payd of late."

In her next entry Lady Willonghby gives a glimpse of the way the ladies of the period passed their time, and in the picture she draws are indications of an active existence, yea, an example which might beneficially be followed by some of the nineteenth century drones. To write that "inside the hall was a scene of busy activity, not devoted to a mere carnival," would abash the moths that now play around fashion's blaze. The tendency of the hour is rather more apeish than practical, and the very progress of civilisation, as it is sometimes termed, is only a development of that spirit of indolence which led to the downfall of even mightier empires than that on whose limits "the sun never sets." The Great Hall, with its blazing fire, and the women busy at their spinning, ever and anon singing to the hum of the wheel, must have been a pleasant sight to look upon. "Nancy did desire that she might have a wheel taken to the parlour, much preferring the making of thread to using the same. Margaret is a notable needle woman. Her sister brought a bright blush to her cheeke by some query respecting a particular piece of needlework in hand, and added, on perceiving the effect she had produced, she had heard St. Earasmus de la Fountain much commend the delicate paterne."

"1641, Tuesday, Mar. 30.—When I came downe staires met John in the hall; he had brought me a letter, and had heard divers reports. He had the good hap to fall in with messengers on their road to the North, and accompanied them a mile or two on their way to gaine what intelligence he could. When the Earle of Strafford was brought from the Tower, he was guarded by 200 of the Train-band on his way to Westminster Hall. Every day of the past weeke he was brought to and fro to the Triall. The King and Queene and the Prince proceeded to Westminster about 9 of the clock. They sat in their private Closet, one being enclosed on each side of the throne with boards, and hung with Arras, in order that the King might be present without taking part, untill such time as he should choose, neverthelesse he shortly brake downe with his own Hand, and so sate in the eyes of all. . . There was much Eating and Drinking during the Day, unseemly conduct in the King's presence." . .

Lady Willoughby was evidently of a type superior to the fanaticism that passed for religion in that unhappy period, for she writes: "The Chaplain and I agree not in these matters, and he hath ever readie in his mouth Texts from Holy Scripture to justify Bloodshed. . . . 1641, Sat., April 24th. The Bill hath pass'd the Commons House by a very great Majority, and is sent up to the Lords. Mobs of violent men were gathered round Parliament crying for Strafford's Blood. 1641, May 13. Thursday.

The Bill has passed, the majority 21 to 19. My Husband sayeth many left the House. . . The Royal Assent has beene given by Commission. When the Earle of Strafford was informed thereof, he layed his Hand on his Breast, and Sayd 'Put not your Trust in Princes.' Poore Man, he hath good Reason to say so."

"May 13, 1641. The Execution took place on Wednesday, the 12th. The crowds of people present were orderly."

"Wednesday, Sep. 15, 1641. The King is still in Scotland, but is likely to go to Ireland. Rebellion, and dreadful Massacres in that unhappy Country."

"Dec. 24. Tuesday. The Bishops accused of High Treason."

In her next entry Lady Willoughby refers to those incidents in history which have had so important a bearing on the civil and political liberties of the country; and though sometimes we find a certain section of the religious world, or perhaps we might say with greater truth, that portion of it that subordinates its religion to its politics, claiming for itself the honour of an ancestory that alone fought the battle of liberty, when we are permitted to raise the veil of history we find that not one can cast a stone at another, that not one can claim any pre-eminence, but rather that a wise and inscrutable Providence has so directed the flow of the current in His own mysterious way that the light of liberty has spread, and the prosperity of a people increased.

"April 5, Tuesday, 1642. The afternoon was fine, and I walked with the children to Framlingham. Met there Dr. Sampson. He was in much concerne for his friend Mr. Lovekin, the Rector of Ufford, who hath beene plundered of everything save one silver spoone, which he did hide in his sleeve."

"Saturday, April 30, 1642. A messenger saying he was from Yorke. I did lose no time in seeing him. He sayd the Lord Willoughby had not time or meanes to write, but sent me his ring as a token that he who bore it was to be trusted in his Relation of Affaires as they then were. On the 22nd the King sent the Duke of Yorke and the Prince Palatine with the Earle of Newport to Hull without any armed force, my lord with them."

"July 16, Saturday. The paper says the Lord Willoughby is made Lord-Lieutenant of Lincolnshire, and Mr. Oliver Cromwell, the member for Cambridge is a colonel, and will raise forces and money in that country and Norfolk and Suffolk. Some part of Suffolk has shown itself in Favour of the King. Would that my Lord were at Home; yet his Estates lying chiefly in Lincolnshire, his Presence there is doubtlesse important. Not only have the wealthier sort brought in their money, silver goblets, and such like, but poore women of their small meanes, even to their silver bodkins and thimbles."

"August 29, Monday.—The Royal Standard set up in Nottinghame; the evening was stormy; and the next morning the Standard was found blown downe, and some say it so happened a second time, and many of the Royalist party much cast downe by an event so ominous. Poore King, my Heart pitieth him, as who can help? Happy they who are not set in high places."

"September, 1642.—The King hath marched towards London. The Parliament having notice thereof, ordered the train bands to be in readinesse, and that the city should be fortified with posts and chaines, and they say vast numbers of people, even women and children, came to the worke, digging and carrying the earth to make new fortifications."

"October 28, 1642.—Tidings of an encounter between the two Armies, the first report that our side were defeated, then came others that the King's Forces were beaten with great losse. Certaine it was that a battle had beene fought, and late in the evening I saw from my bedroom window a man riding up, his horse stumbling from fatigue, and presently was told it was Sheppard. As onely from great necessitie would my husband send from him this trusty man, I feared some ill newes, and when Sheppard said his lord was well I could scarcely stand so great was the reliefe from that which I was afraid of hearing. A battle had beene fought at a village called Keynton. Lord Essex, with his army in the village, the King's halted at Edge Hill. Essex advanced into the Paine, and he ordered the artillery to fire on that part *where the king was reported to be*, and a terrible fight began. The Royal Standard was taken. Prince Rupert entered Keynton, pillaging and committing great cruelty. Men sayd it would have gone hard with Essex if he had not thus lost time. My Lord joined them with his Regiment, Hampden's and another in the height of the conflict; they had laid on the field all night, without covering or provisions. He told Shephard to tell mee he could not be in better company, Col. Hampden and he being much together. Some wished to pursue the King, who is gone towards Banbury; others advised rest for the soldiers."

"Nov. 2.—The Lord says House at Broughton hath been taken by Prince Rupert."

"Nov. 18, Saturday.—Lord Essex was in the House, which had just received a gracious answer from the King, and asking if hostilities were to be suspended. Whilst he spoke, he heard the sound of cannon, he hastily left the House and galloped acrosse the park in the direction of the sound, and he found that Prince Rupert, who was followed by the King and the whole Army, had taken advantage of a thick Fog, and had attacked Brentford, where was Col. Hollis's Regiment, who fought so well, the Regiments of Col. Hampden, and My Lord Brooke had time to come up. Essex, at the head of more than 20,000 men, it is sayd, was urged by Hampden, Hollis, and others to pursue the King. Cart loads of provisions, wine, ale, &c., were sent out of London to the Army."

"1643, Thursday.—People say there was a Rising for the King at Lowestoffe, and that Colonel Cromwell, with 1,000 horse, came upon them unawares, and gained the town with small difficulty. It is confidently sayd Colonel Cromwell hath gone to Norwich, thank full to heare the same. I had trembled to think of him within so few miles of us. Armstrong heard at Woodbridge, when he went to the faire on Wednesday, that Colonel Cromwell and my Lord have joined the army at Loughborough and are expected to make an attack on Newark, They say Cromwell's soldiers are the best ordered of any, save Hampden's Green Coats."

"1643, Wednesday, July 5.—Heard at Framlingham that Hampden was interred in the Parish Church of Hampden, his regiment following him to the grave singing the 90th psalme. After seeing their friend layd in the grave they returned singing the 43rd psalm."

"1644-5, January 14, Tuesday.—The Chaplaine is return'd. Another of these dreadfull executions, the Archbishop was beheaded on the 10th. Poore old man, he hath suffered even in this world, a large measure of retribution for his past cruelties. At the end of his speech, when upon the scaffold, he said he forgave all the world, all and every of his bitter enemies, and that no man could be more willing to send him out of the world than he was to go out. Some over zealous Presbyterian did press him with questions, he replied 'The knowledge of Jesus Christ was alone the meanes of salvation.' To the headsman he gave some money and said, '*Do thine office in mercy.*' As he knelt downe he turned pale, thereby proving it false what some were whispering about, that he had painted his face that he might not looke afraid."

"1645.—Greatly surprised to read in the *Perfect Diurnal* that the House has moved that the Lord Willoughby be made an Earle, and the same of other Lords. We heare that an English Barony is to bee conferr'd on Lieutenant-General Cromwell, with an estate of 2,500 pound yearly. An order hath pass'd that the summe of 3300 pounds be paid to the Lord Willoughby, which I am sure the sayd Lord much needeth. [Dec. 9th, 1645.— Latham House in Lancashire is taken, the Lady Derby having defended it two yeares.] The Earle in the Isle of Man by the King's command. For 9 months together the besieged party held communication with their friends by meanes of a Dog, in this way: They tied a letter round his throat, and he went to where he did use to live, 3 miles off. Here he was kept, and when any papers were to be sent his mistresse tyed them in like manner, and having kept him awhile a hunger'd open'd the door and beat him out when he set off and returned to his master, who was in Latham House. He was at last shot by a souldier, but got to the Mote side near the gate, and there died. The House is burnt, the rich silk hangings of the beds were torn to pieces and made into sashes. This history of the Dog was related to mee by one there present." . . .

"1647, June 24, Thursday.—Much discontent rising up, the *Presbyterian* party have proclaimed the establishment of their Form of Worship to the exclusion of every other. My Lord becometh more and more dissatisfied with the spirit of bigotry which has of late gathered such strength, and the self-exaltation as exclusive as that of Popery, which they do condemn in others." . .

"July 25, Friday.—The Army is greatly incensed, and hath broke up its Quarters at Nottinghame, and march'd, people say, upon London. Alas, must more blood be shed? What will become of this unhappy country? No King, no rulers, and a large victorious army set in opposition to the now feeble power of a misguided and fanatic House of Commons. And woe is me! The husband whom I love and honour so mixed up with them that he must abide by their acts and share in them. . . . . Great tumults in London. The Speakers of both Houses, and great part of the Members have put themselves under the protection of the Army. . . . . . . They proceeded to appoint a committee of safety, and the city issued a proclamation to the effect that they desired a happy and speedy peace by the settlement of true religion, and the re-establishing His Majesty in his just rights and authority. . . I did once behold this Cromwell, who maketh so many quail before him, but me thought his looke was hard and cunning, and I liked him not."

The misgiving of Lord Willoughby as to the future of his King is graphically described by his lady—how the Revolutionists in their turns had had their power usurped by the army led by their idol Cromwell, and how, even in that early stage of development, the real patriots were learning to their cost that though they had dethroned a lawfully annointed and appointed King, the power and authority they had sought for the people was merged into a military dictator, whose arrogance was more galling, and whose rule was distinguished by a tyranny far exceeding that which had deluged the country with blood.

CHAPTER XVIII.

AS the diary of Lady Willoughby is replete with incidents and references to a period interwoven with the national traditions and development of national traits, and as reflecting the opinions of those most interested, it would be unfair to the reader to withhold any portion thereof that places the most eventful period of English history in the true light in which it was viewed by those who had the best opportunities of judging. Historic events can only be viewed by their effects, and though, perhaps, no period of the past opens out so wide a field for varied criticism, and none that has been more subject to a plethora of praise or blame, yet only can we measure those important issues to the extent of the information at our disposal. In the diary of Lady Willoughby we have the converged opinion of the more intellectual and more discerning of the age, and though on the one hand we trace the effects of the social upheaval resulting in greater liberty, more tolerance, and the growth of national prosperity, on the other we are led to look above and beyond the tragic scene itself, and trace a "higher power" ere we can allow that such infinite blessings have been evoked. Revolutionary periods are always periods of danger, and though it is easy to preach of a wrong, it is not quite so easy to point a remedy. The fetters of religion were struck off, only to be rivetted the more firmly under the new Regime. The ecclesiastical machinery of a time-honoured church was removed in order to place shackles more firmly drawn around the necks of the people; and religious enthusiasm that had been so powerful an agent in camp and battle, became a danger to the common wealth in peace. That a reaction of the public feeling was beginning to show itself, and that the fear of the victors was developing, was indicated by the hurried manner in which the King was executed.

Under the date of June 25, 1647, we have the following entry:—"The Earle of Northumberland hath had permission to take the *King's* children to see their father, *coming to Caversham*, we are told. A great number of people flocked thither to see them, and strewed the way with greene branches and herbes. Poor children! Their pitifull condition moved many hearts, and no marvel. Many will in secret rejoice that this drop of comfort is permitted to the unhappy King." August 3, Tuesday.— "Voted in the House that the Army should not come within 40 miles of London." Evidently the Army had become a terror to the community, for, in her next entry, Lady Willoughby informs us "They say the Army hath made *St. Alban's* their headquarters, and have sent up to accuse Hollis, Stapleton, Maynard, and others. Great tumults in London; the Speakers of both Houses and great part of the members have put themselves under the Protection of the Army. Sorely perplex'd, and know not what is the meaning of these disturbances, or what may befall my *Husband*. The children, too young for care, are as happy as May Queenes." Aug. 12, Thursday.— "One day cometh and then another, and yet no tidings ; this is hard to endure, ignorant what may betide us in these evil times. Aug. 14, Saturday. Late to-night my dearest love rode hastily up. He was safe for the present moment, and my first feeling was of unmix'd thankfullnesse to Him who permitted us to meete once more. After he had rested awhile, he entered into some relation of the late events in the *House*. He and many others have believed that the power of the Army endangered the libertie of the Countrie and the Common Councill of London united with them, and met, and sent a letter to the General declared their wish for peace, and entreating that the Army might not advance, nor intermeddle with the rights and privileges of the city. The train-bands were ordered out. Some members met in either House, but the Speakers came not, and to my *Lord's* amazement he was chosen Speaker *pro. tempore* and *Mr. Pelham* of the *Commons*. They proceeded to appoint a Committee of Safety, and the *City* issued a proclamation to the effect that they desired a happy and speedy peace by the settlement of true religion, and the re-establishing his Majesty in his just rights and authority."

Thus early was the halcyon period disturbed, and those who had been most restless in their efforts— those who had looked forward to the dawn of brighter prospects in the overthrow of the Kingly power—

found to their cost that the change was only from one form of despotism to another, having greater power, and with less restraining motive to control their actions. "But the proceedings of the House," continues Lady Willoughby, "were marked by uncertainty and trepidation, and the day following, Fairfax came up to Westminster, attended by Cromwell and regiments of Horse and Foot. The Generall on horseback, with his Lifeguard, then the Speakers and Members of the *Lords* and *Commons* in coaches; and another regiment of Horse brought up the rear. Mr. *Whittock* writes, 'The Officers and Gentlemen, and every soldier, had a branch of lawrel in his hat.' The Generall received the Thankes of both Houses, and was made Lieutenant of the Tower, and thus the Army asserted its Supremacy. . . There is one, my Husband sayes, that lackes not the will to become Leader, or peradventure the power, but none have penetrated his heart or know if he may be trusted. I did once behold this *Cromwell* who maketh so many quail before him, but methought his Looke was hard and cunning, and I liked him not. 'And the *King*, dear Husband,' I asked, 'is he safe? Will he depart the Country?' 'No man knoweth,' he replyed; 'he will not be permitted to leave the Country, if Guards and Strong Castles can prevent. He is safe so far as concerns his Life; he may be deprived of Power or even of his Crowne, but on no Plea can they take his Life. And yet who shall say where they will stop?'

This feeling of sympathy, as expressed by Lady Willoughby, was only a re-echo of the feeling of the country. Little did they surmise that this deluge of blood would only tend to rivet the chains more firmly, that patriotism was only the illusory sign, the bewitching symbol under whose shadow greater crimes would be committed. But the dark forebodings were more than realised, and many of those who fought with only the patriotic spirit to emulate and sustain them were ready to say with Lady Willoughby, "I would lay downe my life to know him (the king) to be safe : we have fought and striven; and have set a stone rolling that haply will crush all that come in its way—*Laws, Parliament, or even the King himselfe.*" The reaction on the national mind is thus graphically described, and the barren result, so far as national anticipation went, was so plainly manifested, even to those who had borne the blast of the storm, that Lady Willoughby's portraiture of her husband is a word painting of more than dramatic interest. She says:—"My husband leant downe his Head on the table, and hid his Face on his arme, and so remained overwhelmed by the prospect of Misery before us. I ventured not to speake : it is an awfull thing to behold the Spirit of a Strong Man shaken, and to hear Sobbes burst forth from his over-burthened Heart. At length such violent shivering seized him that I summoned Armstrong."

On Nov. 13th (Saturday, 1647) Lady Willoughby refers to the report that "the King hath escaped from Hampton Court." It is currently believed that some officers of the army did secretly communicate with the King, and had instructions from General Cromwell himself and others that if he would assent to their proposals, which were lower than those of the Parliament, the armie would sette him againe on the Throne. . . . . Some are as hotly against Cromwell as against the King. Nay, some goe so farre as to say he was in danger of being sent to the Tower had he not left London before they were prepared. Nov. 24, Wednesday, 1647.—This being a day whereon the Parliament sate not, the Lord Gray and Henry Willoughby, a young kinsman of my husband's tooke mee to see some tapestry hangings in the House of Peeres. A portrait of Sir Ambrose Willoughby is worked therein, who was Uncle to the late Lord, and Grandfather to Henry. They did persuade mee to be carried in a Se-dan-Chaire. I was well pleased to get out againe, being much discomfitted by the jolting." Lord Willoughby, in the very early portion of the period, when lawfull authority was set at nought, and "England had no King," discovered that danger surrounded even those who, notwithstanding not only their service, but the dangers they had endured, had aided in bringing into power a force that acknowledged no law, nor regarded with respect any Institution. They had fought for a principle, but a faction had reaped the reward of their victory. They had endeavoured to fight with honour. Now the result was in the hands of a fanatical despotism, and almost too late they were taught to recognise that, though " Sowing the wind, they were reaping the whirlwind," and, like the echo of despair, comes the revelation of one who, in all the varied events of the period, had taken a discerning and intelligent interest—"He (Lord Willoughby) can no longer act with Parliament since they will make no termes whatever with the King, and he is jealous that the Monarchy is in danger of being wholly lost and all rank destroyed."

CHAPTER XIX.

THE crucial period in English history to which we have somewhat lengthily referred, shows to what extent events momentous in their results may be viewed by those who had an intimate connection with them, and have the best means of judging. Not only is it a reflection of the national feeling, but it is also a warning that popular feeling cannot always be controlled within legitimate bounds. To set class against class, to preach a revolutionary tirade, requires no special training, nor yet does it need any special cause. In all ages, in all countries, yea, we have the highest authority for asserting that even in Heaven itself, at a certain time, this spirit of discontent was manifest, and history, in its lucid pages, pourtrays this trait amongst the "children of men" in all climes. The fire brand that would consume only the tares often does the greatest destruction among the wheat, and though this eruption in the national calm, this volcano amidst the peaceful surroundings, may be the hidden punishment which a wise Providence has in store, yet, amidst the chaos, the uncertainty and the contrary elements, which in their tiny atoms become a danger, the over ruling hand bringeth out good. It is only in this light that we can view the grand and glorious effect which has sprung from those times of desolation and misery referred to in the previous chapter, and which we have introduced because one who has been historically associated with Rivington through his connection with Shaw Place was a leading figure therein. But this ancient residence has by far a greater antiquity than that which gathers round it through its association with the Willoughbys, and though undoubtedly the Pilkingtons have also honoured the rural hamlet by their historic and renowned name, we must go a step further back ere we approach a view of the parent trunk. We are, however, content to stand under the grand old branches, and shelter ourselves under what we know, rather than dig further in the realms of fiction and romance. None can view the grand old residence even to-day, shorn though it is of its hereditary glory, robbed of its classical surroundings, and borne down to the level of a common farmhouse, without feeling that they are verily under the shadow of the mystic past, and within the honoured precincts of the long dead years. Certainly no whit of its glory was destroyed, or can be destroyed, in consequence of its association with the Willoughbys, but we must look to an earlier period than such a connection affords before we can trace the history of Shaw Place. Its name, given in the old form of orthography, brings to mind a family identified with Rivington and the district at a very early period. The connection with this very old family estate, which the Willoughbys or the Pilkingtons enjoyed was only marital one, brought about by intermarriage with the *Asshawes*, and here we find, too, the origin or rather the true and ancient name of the baptismally corrupt rendering "Shaw."

Richard Pilkington, a son or a grandson of Robert Pilkington, was born in 1486, and married Alice, daughter of Lawrence Asshawe, of Hall-on-the-Hill, Heath Charnock. A branch of the family was seated in Anglezark in the reign of Henry 8th, and from this "Asshaws" sprang the more familiar name of "Shaw," which even now is represented in the neighbourhood. Like many other ancient names, it lost its prefix in the long past, but to this family the old ancestral home belonged long before the advent of Lord Willoughby, and they were residing there when Sir William Dugdale Norrey, King of Arms, made his visitation in 1664. Peter Shaw then registered a pedigree of six descents. Fuller says: "Richard Pilkington, who married the daughter of Lawrence Asshawe, built the Church at Rivington." This statement, however, as we shall have occasion to show, is not strictly correct, but that he assisted in bringing about such a result may possess some shadow of truth; and what perhaps is more accurate is that he assisted in bringing about its conservation and preparing it for religious ceremonies. That a building was erected for divine worship is undoubtedly correct, for evidence is not wanting that some kind of ecclesiastical structure had existed here, but whether recognised by Episcopal authority or not, we cannot say. In the adjoining village of Anderton, at a very early period, we have reference to a church, though within recent years the present elegant Catholic Church was spoken of as the first church in that rural district. The Lords of the Baronies, however much they might disregard the physical needs of their dependents, had an almost superstitious regard for their spiritual wants, and in many districts tradition points to à spot where the people gathered, perhaps within some rude structure, long before the ruthless Norman approached our shores. Henry of Huntingdon says of William, "That he caused churches and villages to be destroyed to make habitation for his deers." When, however, the thunders of the Church shook even the thrones of kings, and in the rude simplicity that followed an age of barbarism—in the very dawn of Christian light—we find just outside, or even within the shaded groves of the great forests, buildings erected and consecrated to the service of God. Moved by the holy zeal which primitive Christianity inspired, every baron and feudal lord, every petty chieftain or circumscribed king, was ready to bow to the new religion, and almost every manor had its Solomon ready to build a house in which the Most High might dwell. We can scarcely think that a place such as Rivington, bearing a name so characteristic of the past and adjoining the great forest at Horwich, would be devoid of such a temple. At this time the clergy were the most powerful faction in the nation, and a religious force that had so far asserted its supremacy and power, as to own one-third of the land, could scarcely be expected to pass without notice a spot so beautiful and attractive in its situation as Rivington, or Raventon. Again, what spot more likely to attract a religion associated with the barbaric ceremonies of the past, and one too that performed its mystic customs within the shaded bowers and over hanging cliffs? The existence of the barbaric form of worship in any district was a sufficient inducement to the enthusiastic missionary to go there and proclaim the simple gospel plan; and when we remember how early the pioneers of Christianity exercised a power over the Saxon Kings we may naturally conclude that a place possessing to-day its "Saxon Entrenchment" and in close proximity to the early known lead mines of Anglezark, must have been early linked with the religious growth of the nation.

Richard Pilkington, father of the famous bishop, who founded the time honoured school, built a church here, as we have previously noted, but that does not altogether dispel the idea of a prior church, for we find Richard Simm, the church warden, and other inhabitants of the chappelry addressing a letter to Bishop Bridgeman in 1628, in which they state "That a claim had been set up by one Thomas Breers to the inheritance of the church and church yard as his lawful fee," on the ground that it had formed part of the possession of Richard Pilkington, and had been conveyed by his grandson Robert to Thomas Breers the elder, the claimant's father. A reply was filed declaring that long before the inquisition taken on the death of Richard Pilkington (1551) the inhabitants of Rivington, Anglezark, Henshaw, and Foulds, in the parish of Bolton-le-Moors, and who were then reckoned to number 500, at their own cost, had built the said chappel upon a little tuft and quiltet of land in Rivington, there to celebrate Divine service, sacraments, and sacramentals, which were celebrated accordingly for manie yeres of antiquitie." We also learn that afterwards "Richard Pilkington made great labour, and took great pains in Dr. Bird, the Bishop of Chester, and desired him to dedicate the same chapel and chapel yard to God, and His holy and Divine service," and that the same was consecrated the 11th day of Oct., 1541. Here we have an early reference to the Church which "for manie yeres of antiquitie" had existed, so that the Church of the Pilkingtons must have covered a previous ecclesiastical site, or it must have remained for a long period as an unconsecrated temple, until the influence of the Pilkington's with the then Bishop led to its being recognized as a part of the National Church. Again at an early period the inhabitants could appoint their own minister—a privilege they still hold, and which is only enjoyed by some two or three other parishes throughout the country. In this privilege, or singular charter, we are led back into the mystic and hidden portals of Rights and Privileges, and however much the ecclesiastical machinery may have been assisted by the Pilkingtons, we must look for this vested right of the inhabitants of Rivington and district to a source beyond even the period of the earliest of this noble house to find the beginning of this ecclesiastical anomaly.

CHAPTER XX.

IN 1628 we find Richard Simm, the churchwarden, and other inhabitants of the "Chapelry" address to Bishop Bridgeman a remonstrance against a claim which Thomas Broers had set up to certain rights and privileges in connection with the Church and Churchyard. A claim, they say, had been set up by one Thomas Breers, to the inheritance of the Church and Churchyard as his lay fee, on the ground that it had formed part of the possessions of Richard Pilkington, and had been conveyed by his grandson Robert to Thomas Breers the elder, the claimant's father. A reply was filed declaring that long before the Inquisition, taken on the death of Richard Pilkington (1551), the inhabitants of Rivington, Anglezarke, Hemshaw, and Foulds, in the parish of Bolton-le-Moors, and who were reckoned to number 500, at their own cost had built the said chapel "upon a little tuft and quiltet of land in Rivington there to celebrate Church Service, Sacraments, and Sacramentals, which were performed accordingly for manie yeares of antiquitie," and that afterwards Richard Pilkington took great interest in Dr. Bird, the Bishop of Chester, and desired him "to dedicate the same Chapel and Chapelyard to God and His Holy and Divine Service, and this same was consecrated the 11th day of Oct., 1541." That a Church, though devoid of the full licence and power which the deed of consecration gives, had a prior existence the indirect evidence of the above plainly indicates, and further proof is afforded by the prayer of the inhabitants, directed to the Chief Ecclesiastical Officer, and mainly rendered operative through the influence of the Pilkingtons, and more especially Bishop Pilkington himself. To this powerful appeal of a mitred brother's co-villagers, backed by the Bishop of Durham himself, the Bishop of Chester was led to bring into full fellowship with the Church of England the little church on a "tuft of land" in Rivington. But even at that early date, the inhabitants possessed that singular power, which abides with them still, of appointing their own minister or clergymen. When was this privilege originated or granted? Was it a privilege that went beyond that early period to which we have historic reference? If so, then the efforts of the Pilkingtons were only secondary and supplementary, and this fiat of the inhabitants goes to prove that however much Rivington may owe to its Pilkingtons, however honourably the name may be associated with the "Raventon" of the past, and however pleasing and gratifying it might be to local patriotism to find their little church connected with such a famous name, we believe they must honour the memory of the good, honest bishop without linking him with the first history of their cock-crowned church.

And here we go a step in advance in our subject, so as to leave no reason for further reference afterwards, by giving a copy of Mr. Welsh's resignation of the chapel at Rivington :—"*To whom it may concern.* These are to certify the Trustees and Inhabitants of the Chapelry of Rivington, in the County of Lancaster, and Diocess of Chester, and others. That I have absolutely relinquished the said chapel, and do hereby empower and set them at full liberty to chuse another curate thereof, whenever they please, in my room, whereof ye have this NOTICE from yr. humble Servant, W. Welsh. Taperly, in Cheshire, June 14th, 1763." The following is a copy of the Rev. John Fisher's appointment to the Chapel at Rivington: "Whereas, public notice was given at Rivington Church, on Sunday, the 11th day of Sep., 1763, for a Vestry or Town's Meeting to be holden at the said church, on Thursday, the 15th day then next following, about 3 o'clock in the afternoon of the said day, for chusing and electing a Minister thereof. We, whose names are underwritten, being inhabitants and housekeepers within the parochial Chapelry of Rivington, in this County of Lancaster, persuant to our power, nominate and appoint the Rev. John Fisher, Batchelor of Arts, of Peter House, in Cambridge, the officiating Minister of the said Chapelry, being residents, to succeed the late Mr. Welsh, whereunto we have caused our names to be subscribed this 15th day Sep., 1763: Willoughby (Lord) Lee Wilson, John Norcross, John Hampson." There are, altogether, upwards of thirty signatures. The Episcopalian Chapel at Rivington, according to Dr. Fuller, was built by Richard Pilkington, father of the famous Bishop,

but having fallen into decay, was rebuilt in 1666, and it is said that the power of performing the marriage ceremony was enjoyed almost with the consecration of the Church. This ecclesiastical privilege places Rivington, at an early period, in a position denied to other neighbouring parishes, for even in the adjoining village of Horwich this power was denied, and only within a comparatively recent period could marriages be celebrated in their own Church without the imposition of double dues, which went to swell the income of the Vicar of Deane. Rivington, however, in the ecclesiastical circuit, was allied to Bolton, though when and how this alliance was brought about in a parish having such distinct and separate privileges as those enjoyed by Rivington it is hard to determine. But the alliance or any authority exercised by the canonical power at Bolton is really more apparent than real, and Rivington is in possession of privileges and powers unique in the Church. These being extended to the inhabitants of Sharples and Anglezark, the inhabitants of these hamlets must have looked upon the church at Rivington as being to all intents and purposes their own church, and this will be more apparent as we proceed. In the Chetham Society's publication, " Deanery of Manchester," we have the following referring to emoluments or endowments :—
"Rivington certif (ied) 28l. 00s. 00d., viz., 4l. from ye old Hall; 10l. int (erest) of 200l. given by Mr. G. Shaw; 7l. 10s. int (erest) of 200l. given by Mr. G. Shaw; 7l. 10s. int (erest) of 150l. given by Mr. J (ohn) Fielding; 4l. int (erest) of 80l. upon mortgage on land ; 1l. 10s. int (erest) of half ye gift of one Broadhurst in 1681 (if there shall be a sound orthodox minister); 1l. int (erest) of 20l. in (the) hands of John Halliwell; 100l. given formerly by Thos. Anderton and 10l. by his sister, now lost, supposed to have been applied by (the) diss (enting) trustees to ye maint (enance) of ye teacher. By a grant of Eliz (ebeth) an (no) R (egni) 8, it appears that this chappel had been built long before at ye charge of ye inhab (itants) and was then made a paroch (ial) chappel to all intents and purposes by the Queen (v) ide Grant made to (the) Gov (ernours) of (the) Free School by ye Queen by authority of Parliament: The church was built for ye use of (the) inhab. of Rivington, Anglezark, Hemshaw, and Foulds, who were reckoned to number 500. The inhab. at their proper charge to find

a curate. This grant (was) made to ye Gov. of ye School; but no power was given to choose a curate. I. Warden an., 1673." In the " Inventory of Goods," found in the churches and chapels of Lancashire by the Inquisitors, in 1552, we find that in "Rivington Church there was an embroidered vestment, with a suit belonging thereto, another vestment with altar things to match, an old cope, three altar cloths, a coverlet for the altar, two surplices, and three towels, two corporases or cloths of fine white linnen, in which the sacred elements were consecrated, a censor and a crismatoire of brass, a canope and two pixies, a little cross with a painted banner of linnen cloth, two cruets, a Mass book, an English Bible and a manuel, two candlesticks of wood, a lectern, three bells, two sacerying bells, and three other little bells to go into the parish with. Two paxe brydes, belonging to the Church of Rivington, safely to be kept for the use of the Sovereign Lord, the King." These handbells were generally rung by the priests, or their attendants, when taking the Eucharist to the dying or attending a corpse to burial. There is another peculiarity in connection with the church at Rivington—a kind of anomaly in ecclesiastical circles. There are few churches that have not their patron saint or that are not associated by name with either some apostle, prophet or event in church history, but the church at Rivington would appear nameless. It owns no patron saint; it claims no martyr as its protector; acknowledges no association with prophet, priest, or king, and, in this fact, there is that early sturdy independence shown which Rivington's sons have ever displayed in the many national trials and difficulties in which they have borne a part. That the church was perhaps more under lay management than clerical an entry in one of the church records is conclusive evidence, and here we take the opportunity of acknowledging the kindly courtesy and urbanity of the Rev. W. Ritson, in allowing us to inspect those grand old church records, which are so carefully preserved under his immediate care. It has been our privilege to look over many old church M.SS. in the past, but never have we found any so carefully, nay almost so religiously preserved, as those at Rivington. The entry referred to says :—"At a general meeting this day, according to the notice given last Sunday, we, whose names are hereby sub-

scribed, do nominate and appoint as trustees for the future management of the stock and other things belonging to the Parochial Chapel of Rivington :
The Right Hon. Hugh Lord Willougby of Parham.
Joseph Wilson, Esq.
Nicholas Walmsley, gentleman of Preston.
John Hampson, of Sharples.
Moses Cocker, of Rivington.
John Isherwood, of Rivington.
Obadiah Morris, of Anglezark.
William Latham, of Rivington.
John Clayton, of Anglezark.
William Welsh, minister.

There are also 12 other signatures.

CHAPTER XXI.

THE "Charter of Rivington Church" is one of those interesting documents which is not only valuable because of its historical significance, but also because it brings before the mind the peculiar traits and explicit phraseology so characteristic of the period, and shows the undying and inseparable connection that exists between the time-honoured Church and that grand scholastic avenue, the famous Grammar School. Modern improvement (?) and modern requirements (?) have cut asunder somewhat the geographical affinity; but, notwithstanding any and every effort, this affinity must exist, and the hand that would ruthlessly destroy the one must necessarily injure the other. The past has disturbed the grand old connection, but though the wishes of the founders have been disregarded, the signs of the times indicate that the hour of restitution is near, and the voice of the pious dead will again be heard. In this ancient Charter it is somewhat strange to see that of the Church incorporated with that of the School; but this only goes to prove the desire of the founders for their constant and irrevocable connection, and no doubt was intended to show the exact relationship of the Church brought into more vitality by Richard Pilkington, father of the famous Bishop, with that of the School directly founded by the latter, and was, no doubt, meant to preserve the patronage and privileges to the founders. It reads as follows:—"And forasmuch as the aforesaid Parish of Bolton is a very large and great parish, and not only the said village or hamlet of Rovinton *alias* Rivington, but also divers other villages and hamlets of Anlezargh, Hemshaw, and Foulds being within the same parish, and part of the same, are six miles distant and more from the parish of Bolton aforesaid, as we are informed by creditable men. And forasmuch also as the inhabitants of the said villages or hamlets of Rovinton *alias* Rivington, Anlezargh, Hemshaw, and Foulds being in number with their children and servants, 500 at the least (as in the manner we are

informed), have builded and set up long ago, at their
own great cost and charges, a chapel in Rovinton
alias Rivington, to celebrate the Sacraments and
Sacramentals in the said chapel, for their commodity
and ease, that they should not be compelled in the
winter, or other unseasonable times, to carry their
dead and children to be buried and baptised in the
Parish Church of Bolton ; or at other times to wander far to solemnize marriage, or to receive the Lord's
Supper. Ye shall no further, That we, for the
Glory of God and increase of His Honour, extending
the affection of our liberality to the commodity and
quiteness of the inhabitants and dwellers of the
village or hamlet of Rovinton *alias* Rivington,
Anlezargh, Hemshaw, and Foulds aforesaid, of our
further special favour, and sure knowledge, and meer
motion, *will*, and by these presents for us, our heirs
and successors, grant to the aforesaid, now
Governours of the possessions, revenues, and goods
of the said Free Grammar School of Queen Elizabeth,
in Rovinton or Rivington, in the County of Lancaster,
and to their successors: That from this time
henceforth, and from time to time, there be
and shall be for ever, within the chapelry aforesaid, sacraments, and sacramentals celebrated,
and other divine service used, and also baptism
of children, solemnization of marriages, burial
of the dead within the aforesaid chapelry in
every construction and purpose as they be done,
used, and executed within the aforesaid Parish
Church of Bolton, or ought to be done hereafter by
any lawful minister, and that hereafter the people
that now be, and shall at any time hereafter be
dwellers and remainers with the villages and hamlets of Rovinton *alias* Rivington, Anlezargh, Hemshaw, and Foulds aforesaid, at their proper cost and
charges, shall find, and cause to be found, from time
to time for ever, *one* discreet, learned, and meet
Chaplain or Minister to serve within the said Chapel,
as also to administer the Sacraments and Sacramentals there unto the said inhabitants and dwellers
for the time being, and for to do and execute all
and singular other things there that belong, and are
known to belong, to the office of parson of the Parish
Church of Bolton, or of any other parish churches of
of this our realm of England, as fully, perfectly, and
in such like manner and form as any other Parson,
Curate, or Minister, having charge of souls within

any other Parish Church, ought to do. And that it may be well, and shall be lawful to the said Chaplain or Minister to bury within the Chapel or Chapel-yard aforesaid the bodies of all them that die within the village and hamletts of Rovinton *alias* Rivington, Anlezargh, Hemshaw, and Foulds, or any of them, and that the aforesaid Chaplain or Ministers for the time being shall take charge of souls there, and do divine service there, and also minister Sacraments and Sacramentals, and shall take in hand and bear the other burdens that belong to the Curate of the said Chapelry in all things, as by law and custom of the Church of England ought to be done. And, furthermore, we will that all and every of the inhabitants dwelling and abiding within the said villages and hamletts of Rovinton or Rivington, Anlezargh, Hemshaw, and Foulds, and within everyone of them may and shall come freely without let from time to time for ever, as well every festival day or other days and times, whatsoever be .appointed for prayers, and other divine service within the aforesaid chapelry to be had done ; and also at all other times in which divine service, prayers, celebration of the Lord's Supper, or other divine service, shall be had, done, or ministered in the chapelry aforesaid, and there to have divine service ; also to pray and receive the Holy Communion, and to do all other things in such like manner and form to all intents and purposes as they shall do, or ought to have done, within the aforesaid Parish Church of Bolton, or to any other church or chapelry to hear divine service,or to receive the Sacraments or Sacramentals,or to bury the dead, or to solemnise marriage, but only to the chapelry aforesaid. And, furthermore, we will and by these presents grant for us, our heirs, and successors to the aforesaid governours and their successors, that the inhabitants of the aforesaid villages and hamletts of Rovinton *alias* Rivington, Anlezargh, Hemshaw, and Foulds for the time being, may have, hold, use, and enjoy within the aforesaid Church of Rovinton or Rivington, and churchyard to the same adjoining, the aforesaid liberties, from time to time quitely, in manner and form aforesaid, without giving, paying, or doing anything for the same, to us, our heirs or successors, by any manner of ways. And, furthermore, of our further gracious favour, we will, and grant by these presents for us, our heirs and successors, that neither this present grant, nor anything contained shall in any wise extend to discharge the inhabitants and dwellers of the aforesaid, or hamletts of Rovington, Anlezargh, Henshaw, and Foulds, or any of them, or any manner of their tithes or oblations. But that they shall pay and give all their tithes and offerings whatever yearly, and from time to time, to the Parson of the said Parsonage, and Vicar of the Perpetual Vicarage of Bolton from time to time, being after the same manner and fashion as they have hitherto been accustomably paid, and given, and ought or should be given or paid, if this our grant had not been made, anything to the contrary thereof, notwithstanding; and furthermore, we will that the inhabitants of the aforesaid villages and hamlets of Rovinton or Rivington, Anlezargh, Hemshaw, and Foulds, or one or more of them shall not be compelled to further burthens by the Parson of the Parsonage, or Vicar of the said perpetual Vicarage of Bolton for the time being, or of the parish of Bolton aforesaid, but only for the payment of their tithe and offerings in manner and form aforesaid, provided always that neither the present grant nor anything therein contained, shall in anywise extend to burthen us, our heirs, and successors with maintaining and finding of any Chaplain or Minister within the aforesaid chapel. We will also, and by these presents so grant to the aforesaid Governours of the school aforesaid, that they may and shall have their own Letters Patent under the Great Seal of England in due manner to be made and sealed, without any fine or fee, much or little, to be paid, given, or done, therefore to us in our Hanaper, or otherwise, for our use by any means. Because no express mention is made in these presents of the yearly value, or of the certainty of the revenues or any of them, or of the gifts or grants by us, or any of our projenitors or predecessors to the said now governours of the aforesaid school, before this time and ordinances, act, provision, proclamation, restraint to the contrary heretofore, had, made, set forth, ordained, or provided, or any other thing, cause, or matter whatever in anywise notwithstanding. In witness whereof we have caused these our letters to be made patent. Witness ourself, at Westminster, the thirteenth day of May, on eight, [in the eighth] year of our Reign, Annoque Domini, 1566. By the Queen herself. The date aforesaid by authority of Parliament.'

CHAPTER XXII.

IN continuing our remarks about the church at Rivington, we must glance at the Clergy List as given by "Piccope" in his celebrated M.SS.
Thomas Hindley, 9th May, 1597.
1644, Mr. — Blackburn, 1644, G.
1647-8, Mr. Samuel Newton, G.
1662, Mr. Blackburn, yeit Samuel Newton.
    The Rev. S. Newton, died 1682.
1682, Mr. John Walker, Mort, Samuel Newton.
1717, Mr. Joshua Dixon here.
1753, John Waddington, Oct. e.
1755c, W. Welsh, M.A., of Brazenose College. Patron, the Inhabitants, P.M. John Waddington.
1763, Oct. 13, John Fisher, of Peter House, B.A.
1813, William Heaton.
1823, James Jackson.
1856, Thomas Sutcliffe.
1878, Rev. W. Ritson, M.A.

As we proceed a few additional particulars may be gathered by our readers. There is one name in the above list, that of the Rev. S. Newton, which carries us back to a period interesting to the historian, as showing the gradual progress which has marked religious development. The "Act of Uniformity" caused the Rev. S. Newton to withdraw, but the place he had occupied as minister remained vacant, and he returned, and was allowed to resume his duties without interference. The "Conventicle Act," as it was called, tested the religious loyalty of the quaint inhabitants of ancient Rivington, and on a portion of the mountainous range called Winter Hill they met in a sort of rude amphitheatre, in which seats were cut, and a rude stone pulpit was erected for the exercise of religious worship. No spot could be found which was better adapted for the purpose than Rivington. As we have before intimated, the inhabitants of this Village of the Lakes have rights and privileges enjoyed by few hamlets or villages. These in the past were greater than they are at present, and it behoves the inhabitants to be careful and watchful, or at a "time when they think not" their birthright may be still further assailed. There is one name in the list of clergy that will be familiar to this generation, for his geniality was "known of all men." We refer to the Rev. Thomas Sutcliffe, the last incumbent. At the resignation of the living in 1856 by the Rev. J. Jackson, who was a minister of singular parts, and had held the living for 33 years, a poll of the inhabitants for the purpose of appointing his successor, in accordance with the charter, was taken. A meeting of the inhabitants had been previously held, presided over by Robert Andrews, Esq., of Rivington Hall—himself a Dissenter—this being the second time that gentleman had presided at a similar meeting. There were two candidates for the position, viz., the Rev. Thomas Sutcliffe, of Blackburn, and the Rev. Thomas Crossfield, of Stafford, the voting being Sutcliffe 75, Crossfield 45. Some little feeling was imparted into the contest in consequence of alleged illegal voting. This novel way of appointing an ecclesiastical officer excited some curiosity throughout the district, and the *Manchester Guardian* noticing the event said "The vacancy caused in the perpetual curacy of Rivington, which will have to be filled up by the popular voice of the neighbourhood, is a somewhat uncommon event in the history of Church patronage. The three last contests of this description were St. James's, Clerkenwell; Kingswood Rectory, Gloucestershire; and Bloxham Vicarage, Staffordshire; there being eleven other places in England and Wales where this privilege exists, including Billington, Bede, St. Stephen's, Cornwall, Newtown, (Salop), Willanhall, Stafford, Henley, Warwick, Burrington, Somerset, and Aberayon." The new incumbent soon became very popular in Rivington and the district, and by marriage, entering one of the principal local families, he was brought more in contact with the world outside his rural parish. He was a genial, kindly, portly gentleman. In all village festivities he was a central figure, and under all conditions, in sunshine or in gloom, he was a welcome guest. He was far more of the Samaritan than the Pharisee, and on the village green, or at the social festivities at the village inn, he could join with his people without compromising his sacred office. He died March 23, 1879, in his 56th year. The Rev. H. S. Pigott, Vicar of Horwich, preached the funeral sermon on Sunday, April 5th, selecting for his text Psalm xc., 12v., "To teach us to number our days that we may apply our hearts unto wisdom." A large number of visitors from Horwich and outlying districts attended. After an eloquent exposition of the text, the rev. gentleman said they had met together that morning under no ordinary circumstances. He felt sure that he was speaking the truth when he said that the hearts of all that congregation were as the heart of one man, mourning for a faithful friend who had passed away, it might be, only a little time before them, but they one and all felt they had lost one whose presence could ill be spared. In the great Metropolitan Church of St. Paul's, London, there was an inscription in Latin—a simple one it was—of which the translation is "If you want a monument look around you." And so if they might practically apply those few words on that memorial stone that morning, they would truly do so by saying "If I want a monument or memorial to the excellence of departed worth, if I want a monument to tell me how much your late pastor was loved and esteemed by you all, I have only to look around." That large congregation in Rivington Church told him how they loved their departed pastor, and how anxious they had been to shed a tributary tear over his quiet grave, as they came to church that morning. Though they might have wept, those beautiful flowers, already placed by loving hands over the grave where his body had been laid to rest, told them that they need not think of death without thinking also of the resurrection, that they need not think of the grave without also thinking of the Paradise of God, where the flowers of His own culture would bloom for evermore. That was not the place for any minister of Christ to speak flattering words or empty eulogium over the memory of the dead, but nevertheless there were seasons when he ought to speak what he felt. If he were to say that their departed pastor had no faults, he should be saying what all of them must admit was contrary to what God's Word revealed to them when it told them "There is no man that sinneth not." If he were to say their departed pastor had no enemies he might perhaps be saying something rather to the discredit of his memory than otherwise; for did not our blessed Lord himself say, "Woe unto you when all men shall speak well of you." But this he could conscientiously say—and he would be outspoken about it—that having known their late pastor for 23 long years, and that intimately, he had never during that period heard one single person — man, woman, or child — speak a word in disparagement of that good man; and when he (the preacher) gave that as his honest testimony was he not saying the very best thing he could concerning him who had passed away? Was he not thereby paying the best tribute that he could to the memory of the departed? . . . For 20 years in regular succession had the late Mr. Sutcliffe been to preach at Horwich Church on Good Friday evening, and many were the excellent sermons he had heard him deliver on that solemn day. The voice that spoke those words to them was now hushed in death. The Master had come and called him away from them, and while they mourned they must not, they could not, mourn as those without hope. They must strive to follow their dead brother in all his excellencies, in his loving kindness, in his cheerfulness, in his affability, in his good temper, in his wish always to speak kind words, and his charity in life. Let them, the parishioners of Rivington, every time on their way to Church and from Church, when they passed, as they would have to do, the grave of their dear pastor, think that "he being dead yet speaketh," that that grave had a silent eloquence about it which they must not, and which he (the preacher) thought they dare not, resist. Standing, as they would do, then, between the dead and the living, let them lift their voices on high to Him who alone could give them that grace of which the Psalmist spoke, so to number their days as that they might apply their hearts unto wisdom. He would conclude his discourse in the words of one of our own sweet minstrels, as he considered the words to be specially applicable to that time and occasion :—

> And such the tones of love which break
> The stillness of that hour,
> Quelling th' embitter'd spirit's strife—
> The Resurrection and the Life
> Am I, believe, and die no more.
>
> Unchanged that voice—and though not yet,
> The dead sit up and speak,
> Answering its call, we gladlier rest
> Our darlings on earth's quiet breast,
> And our hearts feel they must not break.

Far better they should sleep awhile,
Within the Church's shade,
Nor wake until new Heaven, new earth,
Meet for their immortal birth,
For their abiding be made.

Then wander back to life, and lean
On our frail love once more,
'Tis sweet as year by year we lose
Friends out of sight, in faith to muse
How grows in Paradise our store.

Then pass, ye mourners, cheerily on,
Through prayer unto the tomb;
Still, as ye watch life's falling leaf,
Gathering from every loss and grief
Hope of new spring and endless home.

Then cheerily to your work again,
With heart's new brav'd and set
To run untir'd love's blessed race,
As sweet for those who face to face
Over the grave their Lord have met.

CHAPTER XXIII.

RIVINGTON Church, as it now appears, does not possess the same aspect as of yore, when the submerged valley, where rests the principal "water hold" of the Liverpool Corporation, was an undulating landscape, rich in rippling streams, and dressed in emerald green, where the birds could sing undisturbed by day, and the birds of darkness prowl around by night. Close by it stood the famous "Black Lad" public-house, and there, as now, the ancient Grammar School. Antiquarians of repute have found, in the custom which prevailed to a large extent, only a few years ago in Rivington and neighbourhood, of ascending the sentinel hill— the Pike—with the first break of day, on the first Sunday in May, a relic of bardic worship, a custom brought out by our Druidic ancestors in order to worship the "Sun," as he first appears in his glory on the eastern horizon, or perchance in this connection the beacon hill might have been the scene of the lighting of the "Sacred fires" by these ancient bards on the first of May. But "the quaint-looking Church of considerable antiquity" bears along with it associations that in no small degree are directly connected with past civil and ecclesiastical history. The graveyard itself, where sleep the "village heroes," is a study of monumental, though simple biography, the oldest one, perhaps, being that bearing the following inscription :—"$\frac{1616,}{W.B.}$" But how much of antiquarian value has been lost in so-called improvements it would be hard to determine. The old entrance on the south side has been lately paved with these memorials of the dead, one of them bearing the date of 1666. A small brass plate below one of the windows on the right of the pulpit records the fact that within the church itself "sleep some of the Rivingtonians of yore," for the tablet says among other eulogiums the "Bodye of George Shaw, gentleman, who was the fourth sonne of Lawrence Shaw, of High Bollough, lyeth here," and moreover testifies to the fact that he "gave £200 to be as stock for ever

for the use of the Church of Rivington, the proffitts whereof to be paid yearly to a preaching Minister at this Church." He died Nov. 6th, 1650, aged 73 years. Further up the church, and on the same side, is another brass plate in memory of "John Shawe, second son of Lawrence Shaw, of High Bullough in Angleyzargh," and as in many other old churches on these memoriam tablets is the figure of a skeleton laid out in full length, and underneath are these words: "As I Am, Though Shalt Be." John Shawe died Nov. 12, 1627, at the age of 55 years. The tablet inside the church, which records the names of the clergy, is not so complete as that given in our previous chapter, but in juxtaposition it may both be interesting and useful. The first name is—
"Blackbourn" ord(ained) 1644. Ejec(ted) March, 1647. Rest(ored) 1662." Another entry records:—
"Newton put in 1647. Eject. 1662. Ret(urned) at Blackbourn's death. Died 1682. Aged 40." In connection with both these names is associated a phase of local religious history, which requires some little investigation. The first can only be explained in the suggestion that Mr. Blackbourn, a Presbyterian, conformed in 1662, and again resumed and enjoyed the living of the church. In regard to the Rev. Samuel Newton, the date of his appointment and his age at death leaves us to assume that he was a very young man when appointed, or the date appointment was wrong. In the Survey of 1650 the name of the Rivington minister is given as "Rauffe Nuttal, a godly, painfull, and orthodox minister," while Mr. Newton's name does not appear at all. But from "Calamy" we gather the fact that he suffered ejection in 1662, and "Calamy" further states "That he lived for a time at Crompton, and preached as opportunity offered." In the Unitarian Chapel, which closely adjoins, about which a future chapter must be bestowed, we have the information, "Ye Revd. Samuele Newtone, driven from ye Church on Bartholomew Sunday, 1662." How this tablet got into the chapel little is known, and perhaps an accident was the means of bringing it more clearly into observation. More than half a century ago some workmen were engaged in alterations which required the pulling down of a portion of the building, when the tablet was observed, but not till it had suffered a misfortune. The characters on the tablet

were quite ancient. This fact caused certain persons to put the shattered pieces together, and place them in a frame. A valuable historical relic is thus preserved, and no doubt is a sad and truthful memorial of the doings of that dark period. Mr. Newton returned once again to his ministerial duties at Rivington Church, probably about the year 1672, when liberty was granted to the Nonconformists, and, though the demon of persecution once more appeared, he remained firm to his trust and position until separated by death. In the Nonconformist Register, by Oliver Heywood, himself a Nonconformist of considerable note, we have the following reference:—"Mr. Samuel Newton, a N.C. Minr., buried at Rivington-Lane, Mar. 11, 1682, aged 48. A worthy man." It will be observed by our readers that this statement of the early Nonconformist historian is in direct contact with the tablet in the church respecting the age of this Mr. Newton at his death, but if the tablet be correct he was certainly a very young minister in 1647. Perhaps the disruption and troubles of the time had caused even a straining of this portion of the ecclesiastical machinery. His funeral sermon, Calamy informs us, was preached by Mr. John Walker (his neighbour and successor) from 1 Saml., 25. Both the Rev. S. Newton and his wife were interred in the chancel of the church, and during certain repairs some years ago, what were generally assumed to be their remains were discovered. But, as meet for one whose history was intimately associated with that sacred temple, they were left revered and undisturbed. The Rev. John Walker, the successor to Mr. Newton, appears in the "Harmonious Consent" as minister at Newton Heath, Manchester, in 1648, where he suffered ejectment in the memorable 1662, and for a time all traces of him are lost, till he appears as successor to Mr. Newton, at Rivington, in 1682. How an apparently staunch and unflinching Nonconformist could so easily forget his principles, at a time when persecution was raging, as to accept an episcopal and State Church appointment, can only be explained by the supposition that he was a nominee and favourite with the powerful Willoughby family, which, at the time, was the backbone of Lancashire Nonconformity and residents in the neighbourhood, and to their influence and power must be attributed the fact that the Dissenters at Rivington held possession of the Episcopal Church at a time when many of their brethren were verily outcasts on the "face of the earth." At Noon Hill, more often called now Winter Hill, pastor and people often met "for prayer and praise." The Willoughbys had a greater power, and excercised it, than ecclesiastical authority, and even in the neighbouring village of Horwich this influence was exercised to the detriment of the Church's power. In the letter which the Rev. J. Rothwell forwarded to the Rev. Dr. Wroe, Warden of Manchester, complaining of the action of Lord Willoughby, and "ye connivance" of his predecessor, which was dated Bolton, 22nd, 1717, it would appear that this Rev. John Walker had officiated at Horwich Church, and that when, through the exercise of Episcopal authority, he was frustrated, Lord Willoughby had him installed at Rivington Church in order that his Presbyterian principles should be enunciated in the parish where his seat was located. It would thus appear that this Mr. Walker had been shuttlecock of the rival factions, for at Newton Heath, Horwich, and Rivington, we find him at approximate dates. In the uplands of Winter Hill, or Noon Hill, a certain depression or valley exists, and in the form of an amphitheatre, with the canopy of heaven alone above them, was this temple of prayer and praise. Seats were cut in the sides of the hill, and in the centre stood the rude stone pulpit. But even this spot was sacred, sanctified by the sweet memories that surrounded it—for here, more than a century before, so tradition avers, the Deane Martyr George Marsh, sent forth his epistles from within his prison walls, which cheered the hearts of the Puritans, who gathered here from the neighbourhood of Bolton, Deane, Horwich, and Rivington. The sway of Nonconformity at Rivington Church existed till about the beginning of 1763, when, in a consciousness of their own strength, the present rural chapel was built, and to-day, perhaps, no spot is blessed with a happier reciprocal feeling than that which distinguishes these two sections of the Christian Church. Over one of the windows of the chapel is the date given. The windows are mullioned, diamond shape, that brings to mind the period in English history "when light itself was taxed." Its interior is quite in keeping with the exterior, though the rich vernal ivy that clings to its walls gives a natural architecture both pleasing and refreshing.

But once again we purpose to invite our readers to visit with us the interior of this peaceful looking chapel, with its tall and quaint pews. Denied the use of the church, the pioneers of Nonconformity resorted here about the date inscribed on the stone. Whether the "Mr. Walker" so intimately associated with the church history at that time came with them is not altogether clear. The deed is a simple and concise one, but bears no reference to any particular theological teaching, as then, or now understood, but simply notes the fact "That a chappell or oratory of four bays had been recently erected, intended to be a place for Religious Worship only, and for an assembly and meeting of a particular church or congregation of Protestants, dissenting from the Church of England, for the free exercise of Divine Worship therein. Peaceable possession was given. Witnesses Ra.Ainsworth, Jas. Brownlow, Peter Anderton. The minister whose name appears on the Trust Deed just given was the Rev. Ralph Ainsworth, who had previously laboured in Cheshire, and whose name appears amongst the signatories of the "Cheshire Agreement of Presbyterian and Congregational Ministers in 1691." And in Dr. Evans' able and collective lists of "Independent and Presbyterian" Chapels, prepared 1717-29, Rivington Chapel is put down as capable of accommodating 329 persons, and in the first-named year the Rev. John Turner appears as its minister. And this gentleman is also associated with the Parson Woods, of Chowbent, and Parson Walker, of Horwich, in keeping back the "Scotch Rebels." The Rev. John Turner, says "The Memoirs of the Rev. W. Turner," at that time Protestant Dissenting Minister at Preston, was, upon the breaking out of the rebellion, eminently serviceable to the reigning family. Firmly attached to the principles of the Revolution, and the succession of the Crown to the House of Hanover, he left his wife and infant child, and with many of the younger portion of his congregation, joined the army under General Willes, by whom they were, on account of their knowledge of the country, employed as scouts to procure information and to observe the motions of the rebels. In one of these nocturnal rambles Mr. Turner had the good fortune to fall in with, and, being of powerful physique, to take prisoner and bring safe to camp, a confidential servant of one of the Roman Catholic gentry, who was going from his master with some important intelligence to the rebels. For this "feat of arms" he received the thanks of the general.

CHAPTER XXIV.

NO one can visit the ancient time-honoured church at Rivington without feeling the holy inspiration sanctified by the beauty of the landscape, and strengthened by the sweet associations that cluster around it. The past and the present, yea, the unknown future, with its hopes and fears, are as a living panorama to the mental gaze. The mind draws its feast of beauty from the scenes around—the nectar of the sweet breeze, laden with the music of birds, and rich with honey from the wild flowers, while the soul is compelled to bend in meekness to learn its own future at the grave of the grand old village worthies. Within that sacred pile all its stillness—the solemnity of death is there. But the "greater hope" is there also. There is a beauty in the church at Rivington which far outstrips the georgeous cathedral with domes and mazes, while in the harmony that defies architectural skill to replace is a sweetness and power that tells of the simplicity of the Christians faith and the vastness of the Christian's hope. Who could not worship in a church so redolent with the inspiration of the past as that of Rivington, feeling, as he verily stands between the living and the dead, that glorious hope of a bright resurrection, which all within that sacred fane bespeaks? As one approaches the principal entrance he need not fear, stranger though he be, for on the wall is this distinct notice :

All seats in this church are free and open." Here at least we have the Pilkingtonian intention carried out, and a place so common to visitors as Rivington this notice is of great importance, and perhaps the lesson may be taught, and not in vain, that the essence of the parochial system in the Church of England is, that " the Parish Church should be free and open." The memory of the Pilkingtons, as meet it should be, is perpetuated by a memorial, on which is the following inscription : " Vivit post Funera virtus. Richard Pilkington, qui Templum hoc conditit hie Sepeliebatur, Ano. Dni. 1551. et maü 24, tune donica Trinitatis ac. œtatis sux. 66 bonœ memoriæ vir

Alicia Asshaw ei uxor 12 liberos ei pepevit é quibus tres concionatores fuerunt, et Cantabrigiensis à Collegio S. Johannis ae ea vivit octogenaria. Fathers teach yor children nurture and learning of the Lorde. Jacobus istorum filius creat. Episcop Dunelme 2, Martii and 1660, et œtatis suœ 42 hanc scholam; aperuit anno 1566 et Templum. Children obey yor parents in ye Lorde." Some of the tombstones are quaint and impressive in their memoriams. An almost lost tombstone in the surrounding herbage, broken and delapidated, records that "Here lyeth the body f.o. Zachariah Smith, who departed this life the 15 day of March in ye year of (or) Lord 1693." Another, bearing date 1683, reads "Here lyeth the body of Rachel, wife of William Grey, Eccleston." Another close to is dated 1688. Close to a stone of elaborate description is one of the more ancient stamp, bearing the simple chiselled inscription, "1616, W. B." Even in "God's acre" the distinctions that mark life are visible. The simple stone that records the death of some village worthy is in juxtaposition with the more costly monuments. One bearing date 1663 has initials cut in the form of a heart, doubtless intended as a chiselled token of affection. There seems, however, to be an entire absence of the poetic on these rural tablets, the only one we saw, containing the name of W. Moss, of Bolton, bearing the inscription:—

> My race is run, my pain is o'er,
> I'm from affliction free;
> My loving wife and children dear,
> Prepare to follow me.

Entering the churchyard is the marble headstone over the grave of the "Rev. W. Heaton, M.A., of this place, who died 29 April, 1823," while the marble cross that denotes the resting place of Rivington's last incumbent closely adjoins. Even the present respected incumbent has his token of life's trials in the beautiful and chaste memorial to the memory of his wife.

There is a dignity even in the quaintness and straightforward style in which the village chiefs and officials prepared their statements of receipts and disbursements—a style which predominated in all the rural districts around. We give a few for the edification of our readers:—

"June the 16th, 1732.—John Henry Ainsworth, chappel warden of Rivington, made his accounts as ffoll., and served the office for Roger Simm, of Anglezarch, for ye year 1731.

Received by a tax	03 14	04
Received from Mr. Sweetlove and John Isherwood two yeares Interest	01 04	00
Recd. for a Burying	00 02	00
Recd. in all	05 00	04
Disburst, as appears by a note of p'ticulars	04 07	11-2
Remains and paid to the succeeding Church Warden	00 12	04-2

Allowed by us, John Hamer, Thomas Brownlow, John Isherwood, Moses Cocker. . . June 23rd, 1733. James Simm, Chappell Warden for Nicholas Brownlow for year last past, makes his accounts as ffollows:—

Received by a tax in Rivington and Anglezarch and Chris. Brownlow	03 13	05-2
Received the interest of twelve pound given for the Repair of the Chappell	00 12	00
Received for Burials	00 05	00
Received off the Retiring Chappell Warden	00 12	4
	05 02	10
Disburst, as appears to us by a note, p'ticulars	04 03	04
Remains	00 19	06

Allowed by us, Edm. Sweetlove, Henry Ainsworth, Richd. Brownlow, John Pass, George Brownlow.

It would be interesting to know how many interments are included in the 5s. received for burials. But whether only one, or embracing a number, the economy which characterised our forefathers is exhibited. Funeral reform is one of those social needs that requires to be grappled with. For in the present routine the cost comes heavily on the poor, and what with fees, dues, and the extras ;which the follies of civilisation have introduced the " last dread duty" is dearest of all. "God's Acre" is really the spot where all the elements of a "trade transaction" are present, and the keenest of human sorrows is led to feed human avarice. But death is no respecter of persons, and why should human vanity try to create a distinction where the Great Leveller has levelled all? We pass on to another of these quaint accounts.

July the 4th, 1734. James Simm, Churchwarden for the Moor, has for the year last past made his account as follows:—

Received by a tax in Rivington, Anglezarch, and Thomas Bromley	02 09 00
Received the interest of twelve pound given for the repair of the Chappell	00 12 00
Received off the Retiring Churchwarden	00 19 06
	04 00 06
Disburst as appears to us by note of p'ticulars	03 08 08
Remains	00 11 04

Allowed by us Edm. Sweetlove, John Bain, &c.

The next account for 1735 in which the sum of 00 03 00 were received for burials were allowed for the taxpayers by John Morris, John Hampson, and Moses Cocker. The following entry introduces the name of an old Rivington family; and even this generation is well acquainted with the strange sayings and jocular remarks of "Owd Dicky Latham," and his quaint old Dame Rachel. May 31st, 1739, Henry Latham, Chapel Warden for Rivington, for his house at Dean Wood for the year last past. His account this day settled as follows:—

Received from the inhabitants of Rivington, Anglezarch, and Bromley	02 09 00
From old Churchwarden	00 03 00
Received of George Brownlow for old flags	00 03 00
	02 15 00
Disburst as hath been made fairly, to appear by a note p'ticulars	02 18 06
Out of pocket	00 03 06

Allowed by us, Robert Hampson, Thomas Morris, John Hampson, &c.

CHAPTER XXV.

IT is perhaps desirable at this point to give the more early Churchwardens of Rivington and the districts associated with it :

1692—Thomas Morris, of Anglezarch.
1693—John Darbyshire, of Rivington.
1694—John Simm, of Rivington.
1695—John Simm, of Rivington.
1696—John Abbott, of Anglezarke.
1697—Thomas Reynolds for Mr. Briers.
1698—Thomas Entwistle, of Higher Knowl.
1701—Thomas Whalley, of Great House.
1702—Robert Cocker, of Great House.
1703—Richard Leigh, of Great House.
1704—Thomas Mather, of Jepsons in Anglezarke.
1705—George Brown, of Rivington.
1706—Henry Critchlor, of Rivington.
1707—Adam Pendlebury, of Lostock.
1708—Richard Leaster, of Anglezarke.
1709—James Worsley, of Rivington.
1710—W. H. Sweetlove, of Rivington.
1711—Roger Thropp, of Lostock.
1712—Roger Thropp, of Stone House, in Anglezark.
1713—John Nightingale, of Rivington.
1714—John Finch, of Jepsons, in Rivington,
1715—John Leigh, of Lostock.
1716—John Morris, of Jepson's, in Anglezarke.
1717—John Brownlow, at Moor Edge.
1718—William Sharples, for Ainsworth's, Rivington.
1719—Richard Snape, for Anglezarke.
1720—James Simm, for Peter Finch, Rivington.
1721—James Simm, for Peter Leigh, Rivington.
1722—John Wilson, for Anglezarke.
1723—Will. Sharples, for Bridle's Tenement.
1724—Will. Sharples, for Pilkington's.
1725—John Morris, for Brooke House.
1726—John Hamer, for Rivington.
1727—W. Sharples, for Bradley's.
1728—Thomas Mather. for John Woodcock, Anglezark.
1729—Thomas Mather, for Mr. Turner, Anglezark.
1730—John Sefton, for New House, Rivington.

1731—Henry Ainsworth, for Chapel Warden, Rivington.
1732—Henry Ainsworth, "Chapel Warden," Rivington.
1733—James Simm, "Chapel Warden."
Here the list of names is interlaced with the following memorandum :—
    This year a tax amounting to ... 03 13 05
        Disburst 04 03 04
        Remains 00 19 06
This arithmetical enigma we shall leave over.
1734—James Simm, "Churchwarden," Received by tax 02 09 00.
1735—James Simm, for Rivington.
1736—James Simm, Recd. for Bur'ls. 00 03 00.—Total 06 04 00.
1737—John Isherwood, for Rivington. Attached is memorandum :
The two years' interest of £12 for 1736-1737 was allowed to be laid out in the exchange of the "Communion Plate."
1738—James Simm, Churchwarden for Rivington.
1739—Henry Latham, Churchwarden for Rivington.
1740—James Simm, for George Halliwell.
1741—James Simm, for Mr. Breers.
1742—Mr. Andrews, for Old Hall.
Here we have the first mention of the "Andrews" which became afterwards known as "Squire Andrews," the property having passed to him by purchase.
1743—James Simm, for John Bromleys within Sharples.
1744—John Bate, for Rivington.
    Attached we find the following memorandum, "No interest has been allowed for roof money."
1745—James Simm for Rivington.
1746—Richard Brownlow.
1747-8—John Isherwood.
1749—Thomas Foster for Rivington.
    Memorandum, Oct. 7, 1749. At a General Meeting of the inhabitants of ye Chapelry of Rivington, Notice of first being made publick on Sunday, Oct. 1st, "It was unanimously agreed to allow Thomas Foster, present Chapel Warden, a Ley through the Chapelry, amounting to £8 or thereabouts."

1750-4—Thomas Foster, Chapel Warden for Rivington.
1755-8—W. Latham. Lord Willoughby at this period would seem to be taking a more than ordinary interest in the affairs of the Chapelry, as his name frequently appears as "Assenting Signator" to the "Churchwarden's Accounts."
1759—James Darbyshire, Chapel Warden for Mr. Roscoe's tenement.
1760—William Latham.
1761—Thomas Devenport.
1762-4—William Latham, the latter year for James Brownlow.
1765—William Latham, for "Old Knows." (Knowl.)
1766—William Latham, for Joseph Lee and Thomas Smith.
1767—William Latham, for George Brown.
1768—William Latham. The information is conveyed in a note, and refers to a family that allied to the Willoughby's have been directly connected with Rivingtonian history. He served for Mr. Shaw's House, known by the name of "Johnson's," and for George Brown's House "Called Old Will's," and Latham's tenement, jointly.
1769—John Clayton for Roger Lester in Anglezarke.
1770-1—John Clayton for George Brown "Grit."
1772-3—Thomas Grundy for Stones' House. In the appointment of Mr. Grundy the name of Robert Andrews, as assenting signator, now appears, he, doubtless, having taken up his residence on his newly purchased property.
1774—Jonathan Kershaw, Chappel Warden for Rivington. The following Memorandum also appears amongst the "Church Warden's Records":—"Whereas there were £12 left for the repair of the Parochial Chapelry of Rivington, and on account of the Hazard of putting out so small a sum, it was thought proper by the Trustees of the Chapelry to lay it out on a house for the use of the Curate of the said Chapelry. And, whereas, the interest has not been paid for some years, which, together with the above-mentioned sum of £12, will make up the sum of

£16, it is this day agreed betwixt the inhabitants of the Chapelry of Rivington, at a Vestry Meeting, and the Rev. John Fisher, the present Curate, that he, the said John Fisher, will pay a eleven shillings a year from the date hereof, so long as he continues Curate of the said Chapelry.—John Fisher, Robert Andrews, John Norcross." July the 4th, James Simm, Church Warden for the "Moor," has, for the last year past, made his Accounts as follow :—

Received by a tax in Rivington, Anglezark, and
    Thomas Bromilow 02 09 00
Received the interest of £12, given for the
    repair of the Chapel 00 12 00
Received of the Retiring Church Warden...00 19 06

                                            04 00 06
Disburst as appears to us by note p'ticulars..03 08 08

        Remains 00 11 04
        Allowed by us Edm. Sweetlove.
            "   "   John Bain.
The next accounts for 1735, in which appears
    the sum of 00 03 00
        Received for Burials.
This account is allowed by Ed. Sweetlove, John Morris, John Hampson, &c.

May 31st, 1739.—Henry Latham, Chapel Warden for Rivington, for his house at Dean Wood for the year last past, his account this day settled as ffolls.:
Bromilow..00 09 00
Received from Old Churchwarden 00 03 00
1775—Lawrence Lucas for William Miller, Chapel Warden.
1776—Lawrence Lucas for John Nightingale, "Brown Hill."

[Here we find a more modern system introduced in keeping the Churchwardens' accounts, and the expenditure and income more clearly defined.]
Received from a tax....:........................£6 3 1
Disbursed May 11th—At a Parish Meet-
    ing 0 5 0
Disbursed May 15th—Proctor's Fees 0 8 0
Disbursed May 27th—Seven Quarts of
    Red Wine, at 1/6.......................... 0 10 6

Disbursed Oct. 5—For Glazing Windows...	0	0	7
Disbursed Oct. 7—To Lime and Hair, Pointing, Whitewashing, and Sewing 1½ Day	0	3	9
Disbursed Oct. 23—Proctor's Fees	0	3	6
Disbursed Oct. 23—Presentment at ye same time	0	0	6
Disbursed Jan. 15—To an Almanack	0	0	6
Disbursed Feb. 27—To a Key for the Library	0	0	3
Disbursed Feb. 27—To tread (Thread)	0	0	8
Disbursed Ap. 15—To 3 Stair Mats and a Straw one	0	2	1
Disbursed Ap. 15—To Signing Briefs	0	2	0
Disbursed Ap. 15—To Fencing Yard round	0	1	0
Disbursed Ap. 15—To Clerk's Wages	1	6	0
Disbursed Ap. 15—To Surplice Dues	0	8	0
Disbursed Ap. 15—To Copying Register and Writing Accounts	0	2	6
Disbursed Ap. 15—Rec. of George Brownlow for Old Flags	0	3	0
	2	15	0
Disbursed as hath been made fairly to appear	2	18	6
Out of Pocket	0	3	6

Allowed by us, Robert Hampson, Thomas Morris, John Hampson.

With this entry an entire change in the mode of entry and in the style of writing is seen. The figures are plain, and the caligraphic signs are such as would do credit to any clerk of the present day. We also find that the surplus cypher is dispensed with. The design of the good bishop had been fulfilled, and evidently in that rural village good use was made of the free gift of Rivington's famous son. Perhaps, if a careful investigation were made into the origin of what afterwards proved, to many, an odious tax, it would be found that this voluntary taxation for Church purposes was really the primary introduction of what became a legal demand under the name of Church Rates. Here we have the voluntary mode so far as vestry or town authority went. But this was the *modus operandi* in all such legal impositions:

"Rivington, June 5th, 1751. At a General Meeting of the Inhabitants of the Chapelry of Rivington, notice first being made in public on Sunday last, it was unanimously agreed to allow Thomas Foster, the present Chapel Warden, half a Ley, amounting to 4 pounds or thereabouts, towards defraying all necessary repairs of the said Chapel. Witness our hands, John Waddington, Obadiah Morris, Will. Latham."

CHAPTER XXVI.

THE manners and customs of our forefathers are apt to be thoughtlessly criticised even by those who have no claim to any superior intelligence, but who are only the slaves of a system that has been developed out of the principle which those sturdy veterans practised. And if we claim a superior system to-day we must remember that it is only a natural growth, a change of form, for which even the parties themselves are not responsible. In the Churchwarden's account for May 17, 1758, we find that James Garstang had made a mistake of 3s. 9d., caused by "paying the shot." In this expression we have a broad explanation, and one that will be readily understood as referring to debts owing on account of ale or spirits, a term employed even to-day. It will be as well to remember, though few of our older readers will need any reminder, that even within the space of a few years past, at all "towns' meetings" in Horwich, a certain sum was allowed to be expended in refreshments at the Black Bull and Brown Cow, these two hostelries being near the place of meeting, and patronised by the great officials of the town—for they were verily great in those days—and a town's meeting was the recognised symbol of a "good spree." Even the superior officers of the "Village State" did not think themselves above fraternising with the general public, and an employer, or the village squire, thought it no loss of dignity to drink his pewter in company with his workmen. The churchwardens, as they perambulated the village, carrying their silver-mount"d staffs, thought it no sin to call at the "Bull and have a "wee drop" for their "stomach's sake" ere they marched through the village accompanied by the village constable, and if in these rounds some unluckly one was found disregarding the sanctity of the Sabbath, they very summarily disposed of the case by having him placed in the stocks for a given period—no 5s. and costs in those days. To-day the old stocks in Rivington are in a good state of preservation, and closely adjoining the vicarage, while those in Horwich, in the centre of "Stock's Pad," have been transformed into a seat, where the wayfarer may rest awhile. The following are some extracts from the churchwardens' accounts:

1777—John Shaw, chapel warden for Jephson's, Rivington, and Obadiah Morris, in Anglezark, the sum of 6s. 8d., received for burials.

Spent at parish meeting	0	5	0
Paid Proctor at Bolton	0	8	0
To three gallons of wine	0	18	4
Proctor's fees at Bolton	0	4	6
Glazing church windows	0	3	6½
Signing briefs	0	2	0
Two forms of prayer	0	1	4
Proctor at Bolton	0	8	0
Will Latham, clerk	1	17	7
Proceedings at Bolton	0	3	6
Sacramental bread	0	0	2
James Shaw, for churchyard fence	0	2	6
Four bottles of wine	0	12	4½
A sheet of parchment	0	3	6
Will Latham's bill	1	17	7
Signing briefs	0	2	0
To my journey to Manchester	0	2	6

1778—John Shaw for Jephson's.
1779—Will Latham for Mr. Brownlow's Moor Edge.
1780—Will Horrocks for Isherwoods.
1781—Will Latham for Thomas Wilson, Anglezark.
1782—John Wilcocks for Finch's Land.
1783—W. Latham for John Brownlow " Wards."
1784— ,, ,, Brook House.
1785—Henry Berry for Anderton's Tennement.
1786—Will Latham for Mrs. Shaw, for her house called " Pilkington's."
1787—Will Latham for W. Burton, " Garnets," Anglezark.
1788—Will Latham for Charles Shaw, Rivington.

Under date the 11th day of Dec., 1788, the following appears :—" At a public meeting of the inhabitants of Rivington, otherwise Rovington, in the County of Lancaster, this day held in the Parochial Chapel of Rivington aforesaid, in pursuance of public notice for that purpose previously given in the said Parochial Chapel of Rivington, on the 13th Nov., last past, for the purpose of taking into consideration the propriety and legality of the nomination and appointment of Samuel Waring to be Head School Master of the FREE GRAMMAR SCHOOL of Rivington, otherwise Rovington aforesaid. The *inhabitants*, convinced that the said nomination and appointment of the said Samuel Waring to be School Master aforesaid is illegal, and not warranted by the 'Statutes of the said school, he, the said Samuel Waring, being under the age of 24 years, and not being in *Holy Orders*, and resolved that proceedings be taken as thought fit, to set aside the said nomination and appointment of the said Samuel Waring to the place or office of School Master as aforesaid ; and that another fit and proper person, duly and legally qualified according to the said statutes and ordinances, be appointed Head Master of the said school in the room and place of the Rev. John Norcross, late Head Master of the said Grammar School ; and not the said Samuel Waring." The signatories are Robert Andrews, John Fisher, W. Latham, W. Wild, (agent to Sir Frank Standish, Bart.,) Obadiah Morris, Thos. Norcross, John Kershaw, James Magnall, J. Wilcock, &c.

A meeting was most probably held, for we find " That the Trustees of the said School are requested to keep the School door locked and shut against the said Samuel Waring untill the business of the schoolmaster mentioned in the resolution be determined." The inhabitants of Rivington were jealous of their rights and privileges then, and how much like a satire upon the action and determination of the villagers of the past does the school present to-day.

" Weathercocks " at this period would seem to have been looked upon not so much in the light of present day opinion, but as serving and securing both the ornamental and the useful, and we find in many old records that a more carful scrutiny and observation of their position, and a study of their fixedness or movability was considered indicative of fine, or changeable weather ; hence it was that due care was exercised in keeping them bright and clean, and in such a position as to be most easily observed. Here we have a direct reference : " It was unanimously agreed at a vestry meeting, held the second day of June, 1791, that a weather cock be fixed to the cupola of the church, and that the said cupola be painted white. And likewise a stone pike fixed in the east end of the church, also painted white. The windows also to be painted white.—R. ANDREWS, JOHN FISHER."—The list of churchwardens at this period is appended :—

1792.—Richard Hough, Churchwarden for Rivington.
1793.— "   "
1794.—R. Latham   " (A ley for £8 allowed).
1795.— "   "
1796.—Edward Whewell "
1797.—Joseph Pimbley "
1798.—Thomas Hart   "

Modern singers may learn how far musical talent was appreciated by our forefathers from the fact that in the churchwardens' accounts they appear as being unpaid. But we shall find that a change for the better was ere long introduced. On the occasion of the anniversary sermons the districts formed a kind of "Mutual Aid Choral Society," and the singing in those days was far more demonstrative than at present. Organs had not come into popular use, and all the instruments in the village, and sometimes of the adjoining villages, were requisitioned, and some of the old worthies would carry their double basso fiddle and other musical instruments for miles, their only reward being a tea at the close of the service. We may talk of the noise of the Salvation Army Band, but almost all the instruments in the locality, in the early days of school sermons, were pressed into action, and the greater the noise the more sympathy was evoked. In those days the female singers appeared in spotless white, arrayed in white caps, and resembled very much present day confirmees. Later, however, some little value was attached to the services of the singers, as will be seen below :—

1799—Peter Rothwell, Churchwarden for Rivington.
1800—W. Dandy   "   "
  Whether there was a turn-out of the choir or not we cannot say ; but this year 2s. 6d. is found in the Churchwardens' Accounts as " Paid to Horwich Singers,"
1801—Alexander Gerrard, Churchwarden for Rivington.
  Rivington Singers are allowed 5s., while at the Town's Meeting 10s. are allowed for liquor.
1803—John Walkden, Churchwarden for Rivington.
  In this year is seen a stroke of liberality, 4s. being allowed for Blackrod Singers,

and 1s. 8d. is paid for a "Moore's Almanack."
1804—John Walkden, Churchwarden for Rivington
1805—James Naylor, ,, ,, ,,
1806—Charles Shaw, ,, ,, ,,
In this year's Churchwardens' Accounts we find 7s. 6d. entered as the cost of entertaining Horwich singers.
1807—James Hope, Churchwarden for Rivington.
This year the vestry meeting was held at the Black Lad, 10s. 6d. being expended in liquor.
1808—John Isherwood, Churchwarden for Rivington.
1809—W. Horrocks, ,, ,, ,,
1810—Bannister Derbyshire, ,, ,,
1811—John Foster, ,, ,, ,,
This year Dean Church Singers were paid 10s.
1812—Thomas Lee, for Ward's, Rivington.
1813—Samuel Pilkington, for Rivington.
This year was rendered more remarkable owing to the Rev. W. Turner being appointed minister at a public meeting held Oct. 24th, 1813. Another interesting item is "Postage of a Bolton letter 6½d."
1814—John Hodkinson, Churchwarden.
In the accounts for this year the sum of £1 14s. 3d. for Minister and Warden attending Bishop's Visitation at Manchester.

CHAPTER XXVII.

IN the last chapter we have a reference to the Andrews of Rivington, and though not hereditarily connected with Rivington, they had, for a century at least, taken a more than ordinary share in the government of the village. The Manor of Rivington was sold to Robert Lever, of Darcy Lever, a representative of the ancient Lever family, whose only daughter married Robert Andrews. Thus the Rivington estates passed by purchase into their hands. Ere we step further, it would be well to remember the manners and customs of our forefathers, and mark the development of that freedom which is so conspicuous in our history. Few of us care to enquire how many laws that now hold sway in our statute book were in operation then, and how many were promulgated when "Society" did not exist, and the "Rights of Man" and the privileges of the citizen were neglected. But a time is rapidly approaching when the *Vox Populi* will be the *Vox Dei*, and neglected rights and privileges will once more be protected. In our rural districts, and where "common lands" abound, this resurrection of principle is obviously demanded. Public roads, which through the paucity of inhabitants are little used, are labelled "private roads," and common lands, where the narrow, almost disused, roads point to the numerous inlets or low gates which gave the inhabitants of a district free pasture on these moorland wilds, and even the beacon hill, with its square towers, are emblems of its national character, and the sign manual of its ownership—where the inhabitants of the district have held their carousals, and claimed it as their own headland, whence the eye could drink in the beauties of the landscape around, and the inhabitants, like their forefathers, watch the orb of day rise majestically from his bed. Even here, the high stone wall, with no provision for the pedestrian to mount its time-honoured slopes, would forbid the claims which centuries have endorsed. In some of these more modern actions we discover the relics of a period which demanded "That the stranger, when travelling, should he have cause to leave the highway, should shout out or blow a horn," otherwise he was liable to be taken and treated as a thief, and his redemption could alone be secured on the payment of a heavy fine. These laws were intended not only to protect, but to assist in the securing and enclosing of lands to which the inhabitants of a district had a common right.

Churchwardens, in the more early periods, had well defined and onerous duties to perform. The village constable and the village churchwarden were important officers, to whom were relegated, along with the justices, the due carrying out of the law. In the 12th Richard II, cap. 7, 1388, a labourer was prohibited from departing from the hundred or town where he dwelt without a testimonial ; and in 22nd Henry VIII, cap. 12, 1531, these important local officers were called upon to assign to the impotent poor the limits within which they were to beg. This law was zealously guarded by the indigent poor themselves, who looked upon a certain district in much the same way as the sportsman did upon his preserves, and in some of our local inns we find pictures representing scenes between two well-known men of this type, Charley and Peter, the former preparing to resist the invasion of Peter, and to do battle for his rights and privileges. The visits of these endowed beggars were always to time, and whatever was in their line was carefully laid aside for them. The scene depicts one of these worthies disputing on the borders of the village of Horwich the authority of the other to enter. Peter claimed the right of birth, or hereditary claim, and perhaps in this he was legally right, for by Statute of I. Edward, 6th, cap. 3, 1547, the officers are directed to convey " the impotent poor, on horseback, cart, or chariot, to the next constable, and so from constable to constable till they are brought to the place where they were born, or most conversant with, for the space of three years, there to be nourished of alms." In the 2nd year of Charles II. another law was enacted as follows :—" That any individual, upon the warrant of two justices, on the suggestion of the overseers, were liable to be placed under control, and forcibly carried, or driven by the cart whip, if needed, to the place of his birth." And yet, strange as it may appear in this 19th century, these laws are not obsolete relics of the past, but are more or less welded into the poor law system of to-day in a much wider sense than perhaps we care to see exercised. An old statute reads " Be it therefore enacted by the authority aforesaid, that it shall, and may, be lawful, upon complaint made by the Churchwardens and Overseers of the Poor, in any parish, to any Justice of the Peace, within 40 days after such person or persons coming so to settle as aforesaid, in any parish, in any tenement under the yearly value of £10, for any two Justices of the Peace, whereof to be of the Quorum of the Division, where any person or persons are likely to become chargeable to the parish whence they should come to inhabit, by their warrant to remove and convey such person or persons to such parish where he, or they, last legally, either as a native, householder, sojourner, apprentice, or servant, for the space of 40 days at least, unless he, or they, give sufficient security for the discharge of the said parish, to be assisted by the said parish. Provided also, this Act, notwithstanding that it shall be lawful for any person or persons to go into any county, parish, or place to work in time of harvest, or at any time to any other works, so that he or they carry with him, or them, a certificate from the minister of the parish and one churchwarden, and one of the overseers for the poor for the said years, that he or they have a dwellinghouse or place which he or they inhabit, and have left wife or child, or some of them, there. If the person or persons shall not return to the place aforesaid when his or their work is finished, or shall fall sick or impotent whilst he or they are in the same works, it shall not be accounted as a settlement in the cases aforesaid. But it shall, and may be, lawful for two justices of the peace to convey the said person or persons to the place of his or their habitation as aforesaid, under the pains and penalties in this Act prescribed." The offices of churchwarden and constable were often conjoined, and in some old records the distinction is not always clear, but their responsibilities, and the requirements associated with the office, were more burdensome than modern representatives would care to undertake. We give a list of questions termed " Requisitions to constables, &c.," bearing date 1703, to make your presentments fairly written on parchment, and answers to the following questions :—

1st.—What treasons, petty treasons, felonies or burglaries have been committed in your township?
2nd.—What vagabonds or wandering rogues have been apprehended?
3rd.—What Popish recusants or others have you that wilfully absent themselves from divine worship?
4th.—Have you any unlicensed alehouse keepers?
5th.—Have you any common drunkards, or profane cursers or swearers?
6th.—Is there any decay of houses, or husbandry, contrary to law?
7th.—Have you any ingressors, regrators, or forestallers?
8th.—Has Winchester Watch been duly kept?
9th.—Are your poore well provided for?
10th.—Are your highways in good order?

How would these questions be answered to-day by our authorities? Certain pains and penalties followed any dereliction of duty in any one of these particulars; but, as may be gathered from their accounts, the churchwardens or constables carried out the requirements of their offices. The following is a further list of the churchwardens:—

1815—Richard Pendlebury, Churchwarden for Rivington.
1816—   „   „
1817—Dan Pilkington   „   „
1818—Charles Shaw   „   „
1819—John Darbyshire   „   „
1820—W. Clayton   „   „
1821—John Isherwood   „   „
1822—John Hope   „   „
1823—Thomas Unsworth (Higher Henshaws).
   On the 9th May, 1823, we have a notification of the appointment of the Rev. James Jackson, late curate of Chorley, to the incumbency, and it is signed by Robert Andrews, Charles Shaw, and 26 others.
1824—Thomas Unsworth, Churchwarden for "Old Halliwells."
1825—Robert Andrews for himself, "Hold Hall," Rivington.
1826—Joseph Hayes for Joseph Longworth.
   (This year £2 12s. 0d. was allowed for teaching Psalmody).
1827—John Holt, Churchwarden for Rivington.
1828—   „   „   „

1829—John Isherwood, Lower House, and W. Kershaw, of Anderton's tenement.
1830—Charles Holt and James Jackson.
1831-2—Wright Boardman for Crosses, Rivington.
Here we find a memorandum, somewhat out of place considering its date, 30th May, 1785, as follows :—"There are 3 Locks in the south end of a chest in the Parochial Chapel of Rivington, in which are contained the writings belonging to the said chapel, the keys of which are in possession of the Rev. J. Fisher, John Hampson, and W. Latham." Here, also, we come in contact with another, May 15th, 1811 : " It was agreed to allow the clerk £4 yearly."
1833—Charles Rigby for the "Comp.," Rivington.
1834—John Nightingale, Top o'th' Hill, Rivington.
1835—Roger Gerrard, for Lister Mill.
1836— ,, ,, ,, Morris's, Rivington.
1837—Isaac Bain ,, Roscoe's Tenement, Rivington.

CHAPTER XXVIII.

ERE we proceed further we will refer to some of the benefactions which were bequeathed to Rivington and adjoining districts, and which in the near past proved of great advantage and service to the poor of the locality. These benefactions are not as they were in days gone bye, when by the ties of consanguinity the poor of even more distant districts could claim and receive these charities. They are now more centralised, and, in plain parlance, to ask "How much the poor have been robbed," and how far the "wishes of pious ancestors" have been considered and sustained, is more for the interested parties themselves to inquire into than to carry on the object of this work. But this fact is patent to the most cursory observer, and the objects of one of the charities which is at work even now, when the most careful provision either for the mental, bodily, or social comfort of the more needy classes was made by the worthies of past or immediate days, have been frustrated, their plan disturbed, their motive violated, and the sanctity of the gift sacrificed to the greed of those well able to provide for themselves. We deplore the vandalism that stalks through lovely districts like Rivington, and deprecate and anathematise those who so ruthlessly destroy its rich foliage, pluck up its ferns, and throw down those grand, though rude monuments of the past. But from *whence* has the example sprung? Reprisals follow robbery, and destruction sometimes is a paliative for deferred restitution. When nature's garden is virtually closed to those who have *common rights* therein, and when this *closure* denies them of what they consider—and *rightly* consider—as their birthrights, who can blame them for fighting the battle with such weapons as are most ready and adaptable for the occasion? Their "Sentinel Hill," enclosing the most lovely walks in which their ancestors perambulated without "let or hindrance," have now a terrorising sign suspended, claiming "private" rights, and breathing the terrors of the law. Even the balmy breeze, the rippling music of their sylvan dreams, the holy and inspiring stillness of its lovely glens, and the striking grandeur of its overhanging cliffs, are despotically denied them. Who can wonder if in the near future a change be demanded? In no district in the County of Lancaster has this concentrating influence to the detriment of the whole been more exercised than here. Blackrod (endowed), Rivington, &c. (endowed) for what? We dare not answer. Let those interested reply. There are eight townships interested in the endowment of Rivington and Blackrod Amalgamated Grammar School, and "Shaw's Charity," which amounts to £1,250 a year. The old "Grammar School" of Rivington, and Shaw's Charity had an independent endowment of £950 per annum, and such endowments were for the "education of the poor children" in the districts interested and named, which include Horwich. A sub-division scheme was broached, by which each district interested could have separate aid. This scheme met with the approval of the authorities at Rivington School, and was duly forwarded to the "Endowed School Commissioners" at London, and four representatives were appointed to wait on the Commissioners. But what was the result? After being apprised of the fact that it would be impossible for children drawn from a radius of eight miles, they magnanimously threw out the suggestion of *boarding* the children. Boarding the children, forsooth—the working man, the artisan, the farm labourer, for whose benefit the schools were called into existence—*boarding the children* for whom they were scarcely able to find bread and cheese? Was ever greater insult offered to injury? But the wishes of the pious dead, the Pilkingtons, the Shaws, the Bankes, were set aside; and those endowments, given for their benefit, and over which they had control until the 28th of October, 1873, were merged into one school, whose doors are virtually shut to those who have the only claim to them. The benefactions of past worthies exist only in part, and even the "dow," which cheered many a strayed, but poor claimant, within the memory of some of the present day, is now narrowed, and, we fear, will altogether be lost. In one of the Church records we find the following reference to the Benefaction Fund :—" Benefaction to the industrious poor of Rivington, Anglezark, Anderton, Heath Charnock, to be annually distributed at the discretion of the Trustees in two (2) equal portions on certain days named by Will :

	£	s.	d.
Mr. John Shaw of Anglezark, in 1627 gave	6	13	4
Mr. George Shaw, of Anglezark, in 1650 as stock	290	0	0
Mr. George Shaw, of Blackburn, in 1650, as stock	220	0	0

Which sums of money are laid out in the purchase of lands, &c., as undermentioned :—

	£	s.	d.
Swinton Moor Estase, nr. Manchester, rent	250	0	0
Sutton House (Thomas France's part)	22	0	0
W. Morris' part in Heath Charnock	15	0	0
Ground Rent (Heath Charnock), W. Morris	1	5	0
Ground Rent, Thos. Fairbrother	2	2	0
A "Close" in Heath Charnock	0	15	0
,, ,, Adlington Common	2	2	0
Billinge Carr Estate, Wilton, Blackburn	26	0	0
W. Fielding, Esq., part of Billinge Hill	2	5	0
Moiety at Interest at 4½ per cent.	9	0	0
	£330	17	0

Trustees in 1840, Robert Andrews, Esq., Rivington.
    ,,   ,,   Mr. John Shaw, ,,
    ,,   ,,   Mr. John Wilson, Anglezark.
    ,,   ,,   Mr. Roger Gerrard, ,,
    ,,   ,,   Mr. John Horrocks, Anderton.
    ,,   ,,   Mr. W. Pass, ,,
    ,,   ,,   Henry Milner, Heath Charnock.
    ,,   ,,   Nathan Smith,

In the book is the following "Memoria :"—"Here lyeth buried the body of John Shaw, second son of Laurence Shaw, of High Bullough, in Anglezark, in the County of Lancaster, by whose gift and provision the yearly sum of 10s. is to be paid for ever towards the repair of the Church of Rivington ; and also the yearly sum of Twenty Nobles to be distributed yearly for ever to the poor people inhabitants in Rivington, Anglezark, Hemshaw, and Anderton, in the said County. The one Moiety on Good Frayday, and the other Moiety on the First Sunday in Advent. He dyed ye XIII. day of Nov., Anno Dvz., 1627, being then of the age of 55 years."

"Blessed are the dead who die in the Lord."

At the bottom of the announcement is a skeleton reclining on a tombstone, with the words : "As I am, thou shall be."

In the same book is found a list of books which are in the chest of the church, with the following later information:—"But on the appointment of the Rev. Thomas Sutcliffe only a few were found, which is testified to as witness by Mr. John Howarth." In 1834 we find the following relative to the parsonage:—"The parsonage house is built of stone and covered with slate, four rooms above and four rooms below, a small stable five yards square, part thatched, part slated, a garden containing 825 square yards. The stipend consists of an estate lying in Lower Darwen, called 'Moss,' now let at £63 (since sold and money invested), together with a 'close' at £16. A rent charge of £10 yearly from estate in Heath Charnock called 'Bretters,' £4 by owners of Old Hall, in Rivington; add to the above £7 8s. from Queen Anne's Bounty—now only £6. Burial dues 1s., in chapelry 2s. out, christenings 6d., in chapelry 1s. out. Fees double in the morning; marriage by banns 3s. 6d., now 4s.; marriage by licence 5s.; new grave in chapelry 2s. 6d. and 5s. out; headstone 5s., flat stone 10s. The interest of £12 left by Mr. Shaw, of Anglezarke, towards repairing the roof of the said church; for this 11s. a year paid by minister. Stock: 1 bell, 3 pieces of Communion plate, table cloth, and napkin. The wardens repair churchyard fence; clerk's wages £4 per annum with allowance of 12s. for washing surplice and ringing, 2s. for table linen and Communion plate, 6s. for cleaning yard. "At a meeting on Wednesday, December 3rd, 1834, minister in the chair, in was resolved, on the motion of Mr. Andrews, seconded by Wright Boardman, 'That this meeting do record their grateful sense to Almighty God for the timely discovery of the fire lighted by an incendiary on the night of Monday last, and the consequent preservation of this place of worship from the destruction to which it had been doomed.' After votes of thanks to the parties by whose efforts the church was saved, it was resolved that the churchwarden prosecute to conviction John Simm, the incendiary named. A double rate this year was levied for the repairs of the church." Proceeding with the list of churchwardens we find:—

1838-9—Roger Gerrard for ye widow Pilkington.
1840—W. Woods for Old Cates.
1841—Joseph Heyes for Roger Brown, "Old Rachels."

1842—Joseph Heyes for Tootels in Anglezark.
1843—Joseph Heyes for Lower Darbyshires.
1844—James Bain for Old Knowl.
1845—James Bain for Nightingale's, Anglezark.
1846—William Taylor for Johnsons and Old Wills.
1847—Edward Rothwell for the Crut, Rivington.
1848—Thomas Pilkington for the Lea, Anglezark.
1849—I. Bain for William Smith, Lower Knowl.
1850—I. Bain for Bennett Anderton, Bradleys, Rivington.
1851—John Clayton for Brook House, Anglezark.
1852—I. Bain for Turner's, Rivington.
1853—Bennett Low for New Ale House (Black Lad), Rivington.
1854—I. Bain for John Winstanley, "Gir' Nest," Anglezark.
1855—W. Taylor for Great House, Rivington.
1856—John Howarth for New Hall, Rivington.
1857—J. Pilkington   ,,   ,,
1858—James Ashworth   ,,   ,,
1859—Andrew Berry   ,,   ,,
1860—I. Bain   ,,   ,,
1861—W. Ryder, for Rivington.
1862-3—   ,,   ,,

In 1862 the church was renovated at a cost of over £500. We have repeatedly referred to the Shaw family as we have proceeded, and perhaps no family has, in its ramifications, been more connected with the Rivington of the past, yea, and with the present, than this real old village family. For generations they have been looked upon as, perhaps, the most ancient local family, and this generation will remember the eccentric "Kestor" and the more liberal Walter. At the eastern end of Rivington Chapel, along the outside wall, the "Mortuary Chapel," if we may be permitted the description, of past generations of this family is situated. Here rests Bolton's first Mayor, C. J. Darbyshire ; while the Harwoods and other names of local note find a last resting place within the quiet, calm and rural beauty that clusters around this place of worship. Its grand old yew tree, its ivy covered walls, the weeping willows that bend as in sorrow over the graves, bespeak the spot where, amidst the holy calm, the sweet serenity of nature's own bower, the body may well rest in joy and gladness, till the Archangel's trump sounds above the wreck of elements and the clash of worlds, bidding them wake to the life that never dieth.

CHAPTER XXIX.

IT is always well to take outside opinion, even where Nature has lavished her beauty with no sparing hand. We give in its entirety the following article from the *Manchester Examiner*, headed "Rivington Pike," signed by "J. P. K. :—

Lancashire people frequently travel far in search of fresh air and good scenery, and often, in consequence, overlook the opportunities of obtaining these which present themselves nearer home. They have frequently, we believe, had their negligence in this respect pointed out to them, but it was not till last Monday that we realised what an amount of cheap and healthy enjoyment they miss in consequence. If anyone wishes for a thoroughly enjoyable excursion, at little expense, let him do as we did on that day. But biding his time till the weather is as bright and as fine as it was then, let him take the train to Horwich, and ascend Rivington Pike. The Pike stands out clearly against the blue sky as we come along the line from Bolton, looking singularly near and low, appearances the deceitfulness of which we had ample opportunities of demonstrating. At Horwich Junction we change, and run along the short branch line to Horwich, passing on our way the new works of the Lancashire and Yorkshire Railway Company, which bid fair to change the whole aspect of the neighbourhood, and transform Horwich into a second Crewe. The transforming effects are already beginning to manifest themselves in the village in the shape of new shops and houses; and, however it might grieve the soul of Mr. Ruskin to see the blasting hand of modern civilisation laid upon the old place, it struck us that up to the present time at any rate the changes she has wrought have effected decided and much-needed improvement. We console ourselves, moreover, in prospect of the coming change, by thinking of the much-needed employment it will bring to idle hands, and by remembering that it is not likely to have any very serious influence on what is the object of our visit—the Pike and the view therefrom.

Arriving at Horwich Station, we turn to the left, and then take the first road to the right, and immediately begin to mount. There are several ways of getting to the Pike, but this is the easiest to find, and perhaps, on the whole, the one to be preferred, the road being a good one, fairly direct, and (an important consideration on a hot day) not without some shade. Ascending steadily we pass a small reservoir, then some brickworks, and then the road goes through a natural cutting made by the stream which flows alongside and beneath, the sides of which are overhung by oaks just putting on their autumn dress. The directing and controlling influences of man were rather too plainly visible here. The stream had by no means been allowed to wander at its own sweet will. Doubtless the road had been greatly improved by the change, but at the same time one does not care to see culverts and iron gratings when one takes a trip into the country. A little beyond this point the road turns to the right (the Pike is on our left), and is barred by a gate—wherefore we know not; we suspect, however, that the mansion standing out on the hillside, which we have had in view nearly all the way up, and whose strange, patchy appearance, with a tower-like protuberance in front and a wing behind, the light new stone of which contracts rather too glaringly at present with the weather-stained appearance of the original structure, attracts more than it pleases the eye—we suspect that this has something to do with the presence of our iron gate. We do not go through the gate, but take the footpath straight before us, which leads on to a road whose whereabouts is clearly indicated by the telegraph poles. This road runs right along the moorside to the Pike. The view is already exceedingly fine, but as we are a little pressed for time we do not now pause to examine it, but, putting our best foot forward, step out towards the stile which we can see half a mile ahead. This stile admits to the moor, and from it we can trace the path leading straight up to the old tower with which the Pike is crowned. In seven or eight minutes we reach it (this fresh air and this glorious sunshine cause us to feel a springiness and an elevation of spirits which make fast walking not only easy but almost a necessity), and then five minutes stiff climbing brings us to the top, forty minutes from Horwich station. "1733," says the stone over the door of the tower which faces us, as out of breath, we reach the summit. Who put you there, tower, and why, and wherefore are you boarded up at all your windows, and your door barred, instead of standing open to let people get to the top of you and see at one sweep all round the horizon, instead of, as now, creeping round your base—these questions you do not answer. We do not, however, care to press them, for it is not the tower we came to see, but the view. We recognise, however, two advantages in the presence of the tower, though only the outside of it can be got at; of both of these visitors to Rivington seem to take advantage. It affords an admirable shelter from the strong and not over warm wind which is blowing, and we suppose nearly always does blow, on the Pike; and it presents a large surface on which the British excurtionist can perform the solemn rite of recording the fact that he has favoured the place with a visit—enlightening the public at the same time as to his name and dwelling place. We are inclined to think, indeed (so numerous are the names cut in the wood and in the stone), that even if its short-sighted builder did not originally intend it for this purpose, this was the object which great destiny had in view when she prompted him to erect it. If our surmise is correct, we rejoice to see that her wise purposes are being accomplished, and bid fair ere long to arrive at a consummation. We do not, however, at the time, enter into these speculations. We are absorbed in the glories of the scene which lies before us. How can we describe it? Bathed in golden sunshine, all Lancashire, from Horwich at our feet to Southport by the distant sea—from the waters of the Mersey, glittering in the sunlight, to the waters of the Ribble, flowing into the expanse of ocean beyond—lies before us. It is four o'clock, and the sun is somewhat to the south of west. All the country between and below it and us, and to a considerable extent on each side, is bright and clear; but north and south the haze is rather thick, and prevents us from distinguishing details, though we can make out the outlines of the landscape. Let us look round the horizon. Beginning at our left hand to the south, the haze and smoke prevent us from distinguishing many features. Manchester lies behind the shoulder of the hill, invisible, and Bolton is also hidden; the high ground at Farnworth and for many a mile beyond can be traced, however, while away behind stretches the great plain through which the

Mersey flows, and beyond it, in dimest outline, what from their height and distance we conclude must be the hills of Wales. Turning more towards the sun, and looking between Horwich below us and the furnace smoke of the foundries near Wigan (which itself lies over the hill), we can look right over the plain to where Warrington is denoted by a thin cloud of smoke, and a little to the right and more plainly visible is St. Helens, and a train half way between it and Wigan steams along the plain. Right before us, 20 or more miles away, and, as we have said, below the sun, glitter the waters at the mouth of the Mersey, and beyond we can just trace the dark outline of the hills along the North Wales coast. Liverpool itself we cannot see, but the houses of what we take to be Seaforth or Crosby are clearly outlined against the shining waters. From that point right along to the neck of land which juts out on the north side of the mouth of the Ribble—it seemed a neck to us, and we could look right over it to the sea beyond, though in reality it is of considerable width—we could see the ocean for many a league away, though not as far as the isle of Man, which, we suppose, can be seen at times. We could not make out either Southport or Lytham distinctly, though no doubt we should have been able to do so with a good glass. This, unfortunately, we did not possess; we are describing only what we saw with the naked eye. As we get further round to the north the haze again, to a great extent, obscures the view. Preston we can dimly discern, but all beyond it is indistinct. We tried hard to discover Morecambe Bay and the lake mountains, but did not succeed Finally, our view to the north-east was bounded by a high range of barren hills—behind Blackburn somewhere, we supposed. There is no view to the east and south-east; the moorland rises behind the Pike and obscures it. So much for the more distant prospect. To describe in detail all the nearer objects composing the magnificent panorama which lay at our feet would be impossible. Right below us are the reservoirs of the Liverpool Waterworks, a succession of them stretching away to the right. Their bright surfaces add considerably to the beauty of the scene, though we are sorry to see that they are very low, and one, apparently, is quite empty. Beyond them lies the valley through which the railway runs to Chorley; there is a train making its way down to Bolton. Chorley itself is plainly visible, and seems quite close, its cloud of smoking not adding materially to the beauties of the landscape. On the other side of the valley rises the ridge which runs for many miles almost north and south, the ridge on the further side of which Wigan lies. The town itself, as we have said, cannot be seen, but some large ironworks just above it appear over the hill, and form one of the most conspicuous, if not one of the most pleasing features of the landscape. The ridge itself comes from the high ground lying to the west of Bolton, and with slightly diminishing height runs north— that is Blackrod on its side there—till from a tree-crowned point it with sudden slope descends, and is lost in the vast plain of fertile land which stretches away to the shores of the Ribble; far away upon it we can see the white steam of a railway train which is toiling along to the North. Almost behind the point which forms the extremity of this ridge is Ashurst Beacon, the monument on which we can just make out. These are a few details of the glorious scene, which, beneath a bright blue sky, lightly spotted with clouds, whose slow shadows move majestically across the country, entranced our gaze as we lingered on Rivington Pike. We could have stayed for hours noting the details—the green and yellow fields with their wandering borders of trees; the scattered hamlets and farms; the rich brown of moss and moorland; the slope of hill and vale; the flag of sunlight and shadow; the glitter of shining water—but the wind is cold, and the time presses (for Horwich as yet does not possess a half-hourly service of trains), so in order to avoid waiting till after dark we reluctantly say good-bye to the old tower, and casting one lingering look round the landscape, we plunge down the steep path, and in three-quarters of an hour are whirling away to Manchester, with our heads full of memories which will linger for many a long day of the view from the old Pike, which, as we rush along the valley, we see rearing its head above us in proud, calm endurance, backed by the deep blue of the evening sky, as if it were prepared for many a long year to come to defy the storms which rush upon it from over the western seas."

CHAPTER XXX.

THE following letter from Mr. John Bradley, an old schoolmaster at Rivington, will be read with interest :—" Sir,— I received a paper from your office purpurtinge a designe of a gentleman in Oxon to report the state of the present English ffree schoolis, which paper desires my Answer to, and Resolucon of, Sundry Queries touchinge the free Grammar School of Rivington, which, accordinge to desire is done, and herewith sent to your office, which you will please take and represent as followeth :
Imprimis. The fabric of the free Grammar School of Rivington, in the Parish of Bolton, was built at the charge, and by the appointment, of the pious and learned prelate James Pilkington, Bishopp of Duresme, son of Richard Pilkington, Esq., of Rivington aforesaid, who also endowed the said school with lands and tenements of the clear yearly value of 27l 14s. 10d., part whereof ariseth out of lands lying in Lancashire, viz., 2l 13s. 4d. The remainder ariseth out of lands scituate and lying in the Bishoprick of Durham. Other accessions of revenue by benefactors, the school hath none except with improvement the governors of the said school successively have made, which amounts to not above 6l or 7l per annum.

2. The said school, at the humble suite of the said reverend and pious prelate made to Queen Elizabeth of happy memory, was founded, created, and established by her Royal Grant in the nature of letters patent, bearing date the 13th of May, in the eight year of her reigne, by the name of the Free Grammar School of Queen Elizabeth in Rovington, *alias* Rivington to bee one body corporate and politick of themselves, whereby one master or teacher, and one usher or under teacher, are ordained to continue for ever, as also six governors by the name of the governors of the possessions, revenues, and goods of the Free Grammar School of Queen Elizabeth in Rovington, *alias* Rivington, to bee one body corporate and politick of themselves for ever incorporate, and erected by (elected by) the name of the

governor of the possessions, revenues, and goods of the Free Grammar School of Queen Elizabeth in Rovington, *alias* Rivington, in the County of Lancashire. The names of the Governors expressly assigned and appointed by the aforesaid grant or letters patent were Thomas Asshawe, Esq., George Pilkington, Esq., Thomas Shaw, Esq., gentleman, Richard Rivington, John Green, and Ralph Whittle, yeoman. The names of the governors now in beinge are Thomas Willoughby, gentleman, John Walker, clarke, Thurstan Bradley, George Shaw, Richard Brownlow, and Thomas Rivington, yeoman.

4. Patron of the said school was the good Bishop himself, *durante vita*, and after his decease the Master and Seniors of the Colledge of St. John the Evangelist in the University of Cambridge for the time being, also the Bishops of Durham and Chester, all of which are instructed and authorized by the said grant in some cases, and with some limitations, to choose, nominate, and appoint who shall succeed in the Governor's School Master and Ushers' Office, h.c., when and so often as the Governors of the said School shall faile in and not execute the power and trust committed to them.

5. To whom of right it belongs to visit I cannot say, but 'tis averred by some intelligent persons that it peculiarly appertains to the jurisdiction of the Duchy (Dutchy) of Lancaster, and that it is solely subjected to the inspection of the Honourable Chancellor of the Dutchy *sed de hoc quæra*.

6. The school hath not any exhibition in either of the Universities.

7. Schoolmasters of the foresaid school I find to have been many; but have not seen or heard of anything printed by any of them. A catalogue of their names you may take to be as followeth :—Mr. Robert Dewhurst, M.A., who was appointed schoolmaster by the said patron or doner himself, Mr. Hallstead, Mr. Saunders, Mr. Brindle, Mr. Ainsworth, Mr. Rudall, famous Mr. Bedards, Mr. Shaw, Mr. Duckworth, Mr. Crook, Mr. ffielden, famous Mr. Breares, whose successor I was.

8. Some bookes (and by many 'tis believed a considerable quantity) were left by the patron or doner to the school. But by one ill means or other, how or when its not known, they are reduced to a small and inconsiderable number. Neither is there any library within any town near adjoyning except such as the

school near of Bolton can give a more perfect accompt of then I, from schoolmaster of Rivington, John Bradley. Leave this at the Regester's Office in Chester accordinge to desire, and direction to be communicated to whom it concerns."

We now follow with the "Charity Commissioners' Reference." "In the Matter of the Charity called 'Shaw's Educational Endowment, Rivington,' in the County of Lancaster, regulated by a scheme made under the Endowed Schools Acts, on 30th of April, 1877, and in the Matter of the Charitable Trusts Acts, 1853 to 1887. The Board of Charity Commissioners for England and Wales having considered statements and applications submitted to them on behalf of the Governors of the above-mentioned charity, representing that of the sum of £900 expended by the said Governor in adapting the sites and buildings formerly occupied for the purposes of Rivington Grammar School for a school in accordance with the provisions of the 15th clause of the above-mentioned scheme, the sum of £600 was expended out of income, and the sum of £300 was obtained by way of loan, which still remains due from the Governors, and the Governors have recently raised, by way of loan, a further sum of £100 for the purpose of defraying the cost of providing additional accommodation for infants in the said school, in accordance with the requirements of, and with plans which have been approved by the Education Department, do hereby order as follows, viz. :—

1. With the view of reducing the amount due and owing from the Governors in respect of the aforesaid loans the sum or 31*l* 2s. 3d. Two and three-quarters per cent. consolidated stock held by "The official trustees of charitable funds," in trust for the charity, shall be sold by the said official trustees and a separate order of the board, and the amount remitted unto or in accordance with the directions of the Governors.

2. The Governors may, out of the income of the charity, pay interest at a rate not exceeding 4*l* per cent. per annum upon the amount remaining due in respect of the aforesaid loans.

3. The amount remaining due in respect of the loans shall be replaced out of the income of the charity within the period of 20 years from the date hereof.

4. For that purpose the Governors shall out of the income of the charity in their hands, cause to be paid or remitted to the banking account of "The official trustees of charitable funds" at the Bank of England on or before the 1st day of August, in the year 1890, and in each succeeding year during the said period of 20 years, an annual sum of not less than 15*l*.

5. The said official trustees shall forthwith invest the said annual sums, when so paid or remitted, at compound interest in the purchase, in their names, of two and three-quarters per cent. consolidated stock in trust for the charity, to the credit of an account to be entitled the "Investment Account," until the amount remaining due in respect of the loans shall have been fully replaced.

Sealed by order of the Board, this 12th day of November, 1889,

(SEAL.) G. H. GAUNTLETT,
Authorised 50, 51 Vic., c. 49.

We would especially call our readers' attention to the next of Rivington's charities, associated with the name of a family that has been for generations a more than household word, a family which, setting aside a pedigree which many in "Burke" cannot emulate, have always seemed to have their motto, "Above the people, yet with them." We have abstained from referring to what must strike all our readers, how Rivington's poor and the surrounding districts have been robbed of the gifts which their grand old progenitors left for their special good and benefit, and how much thereof is turned into a channel that is well able to supply itself from its own source. We hear much of the republicanism of the masses, but the republicanism of the classes is a greater danger, and in no place is this more exemplified than in Rivington and neighbourhood. "He that runneth may read" is inscribed on every bye-path, and its beauties would ere this have been closed if we had not a few high-souled gentlemen to-day.

In the matter of the charities of John Shaw and George Shaw, otherwise known as Shaws' Charity, in the townships of Rivington and Anglezarke, in the parish of Bolton-le-Moors, in the county of Lancaster, and in the townships of Heath Charnock and Anderton, in the parish of Standish in the same county;

and of the charities of John Broadhurst and Rachael Charnley, for the poor of the said township of Rivington; and in the matter of "The Charitable Trusts Acts, 1853 to 1869," rule 1 relates to management; rule 2 refers to the transference of all stocks, shares, funds, and securities to be transferred to Shaws' trustees; rule 3, trustees are to be ten in number, resident in Rivington or convenient distance therefrom; rule 4 provides for the old trustees to be trustees under the new scheme, and are as follows:— John Howarth, J. W. Crompton, Richard Shaw, Andrew Smith, Eli Magnall, John Catterall, J. R. Heaton, Ben Davies, E. Davies, and Walton Ainsworth. After further rules in respect to government, sale of timber, mines or minerals, &c., we have the application of income as follows, first defraying all proper cost, &c., the remaining moieties to be distributed as follows:—

Rule 29. One of such moieties together with the income arising from the property comprised in the third schedule to the present order shall be paid over by the Trustees to the Governours of the Foundation established under the provisions of a scheme made under "The Endowed Schools Acts," 1869, 1873, and 1874, under the name of "Shaw's Educational Foundation, Rivington," &c., and approved by Her Majesty in Council on the 30th day of April, 1877, or as such Governing Body may direct to be applied according to the provisions and directions contained in that scheme.

Rule 30. The remaining moiety shall be applied by the Trustees in accordance with the provisions hereinafter contained.

Rule 31. Cottage Hospital or Dispensary. The Trustees may contribute with the consent of the Charity Commissioners such a capital sum, not exceeding 200*l*., as they may think fit towards the establishment of a Provident Cottage Hospital or Dispensary, or any institution of a similar character, for the benefit of poor persons of the above mentioned townships of Rivington, Anglezarke, Heath Charnock, and Anderton, suffering from accident or curable diseases; to the benefits of which no person who is not a subscriber to the funds for the maintenance thereof shall be entitled.

Rule 32. The Trustees may apply a yearly sum of not more than £25 in or towards the support and maintenance of any such institution so long as conducted to their satisfaction. They may also contribute a further yearly sum of not more than £25 in aid of any Nursing Fund or Institution having for its object the provision of duly qualified nurses to attend on the sick and infirm poor of the said townships. The second moiety is as follows :—

Rule 33. The second moiety shall be applied by the Trustees for the benefit of deserving and necessitous persons resident in the said townships, to be selected for this purpose by the Trustees in one or more of the following ways as shall be considered by them most advantageous to the recipients, and most conducive to the formation of provident habits ; (*a*) Subscriptions or donations in aid of the funds of any provident club or society established in or near the said townships, for the supply of coal, clothing, or other necessaries. (*b*) Subscriptions or donations in aid of the funds of any provident or friendly associations accessible to the inhabitants of the said townships. (*c*) Contributions towards the cost of the outfit on entering upon a trade or occupation or into service, of any person being under the age of 21 years. (*d*) The supply of clothes, linen, bedding, fuel, tools, medical, or other aid in sickness, food, or other articles in kind at the discretion of the Trustees. (*e*) The supply of temporary relief in money, by way of loan or otherwise, in case of unexpected loss, urgent distress, or sudden destitution. Provided that the funds of the Charities shall in no case be applied directly or indirectly in relief of the poor rates of the said parishes, or so that any individual shall become entitled to a periodical or recurrent benefit therefrom.

Rule 34 provides for the variation of payments by the Trustees providing they have satisfied themselves that the recipients in respect of poverty and character are deserving of help. This rule also prohibits any Trustee, either for himself or others, to occupy any lands of the Charities or any interest therein, or to supply any work or goods at the cost of the Charities.

The second schedule contains particulars of properties, &c., of Shaw's Charities. (1) A perpetual fee farm rent of £250 per annum, issuing out of a farm known as Peake's Farm, at Swinton, in the Parish of Eccles, in the County of Lancaster, containing 11a. 0r. 36p. or thereabouts, together with mines and minerals.

2. A farm known as Sutton House Farm, at Heath Charnock aforesaid, containing 9a. 2r. 15½p., or thereabouts, let upon lease for a term of 14 years, from the 12th of May, 1876, to Thomas Middleton, at an annual rent of £38.

3. Three pieces or parcels of land, containing 4,390 square yards, or thereabouts, situate at Heath Charnock aforesaid, agreed to be let upon lease to Thomas Middleton for a term of 999 years, at an annual rent of £12 10s.

4. A piece of land containing 504 square yards, or thereabouts, situate at Heath Charnock aforesaid, let upon lease for a term of 999 years to Thomas Fairbrother, at an annual rent of £2 2s.

5. Three cottages in Heath Charnock aforesaid, now or lately let to Nancy Berry, John Berry, and John Birchall, as yearly tenants, at annual rents amounting to £15 12s.

6. A piece of land containing 2 roods, or thereabouts, in Adlington; rent £2 10s.

7. A piece of land on Billinge Hill, at Witton, in the parish of Blackburn; annual rent £2 5s.; lease granted 13th of September, 1797.

8. Perpetual yearly rents in Liverpool, amounting to £68.

THIRD SCHEDULE.—John Broadhurst's charity. A sum of £30 19s. 1d., consolidated £3 per cent. annuities, standing in the name of "The Official Trustees of Charitable Funds." Rachel Charnley's charity: An annual rent charge of 6s. 8d., charged upon and issuing out of certain lands at Whittle-le-Woods, in the parish of Leyland, in the said county of Lancaster, formerly belonging to Peter Heatly, Esq., and now to Miss Mary Anyon, of Gorse Hall.

Sealed by the Board.

CHAPTER XXXI.

BEAUTIFUL in its rural simplicity as Rivington ever was, a change in its landscape view was introduced by the determination of the Liverpool Corporation to make its valley the principal gathering ground for its water supply. The streams that flowed in sweetness from its mountain sides, the rivulets that trickled from its rocky background, and the springs that issued from depths none could guage, were such a tempting prospect that no longer than the usual preliminaries required did they hesitate ere operations commenced, and Rivington was transformed into a village of huts and rude structures, where the hundreds of men employed lived. It is somewhat too recent to refer to any particular aspect of the scene, how amongst them was the unlicensed "beer vendor,'" &c., the lower part of Horwich being also much affected by the advent of these "navvys," as they were termed, and some of the servants of "John" received a rich harvest. These "Lancashire lakes," as they are not inappropriately called, have given quite a charm to the surrounding scenery, and Rivington is the delightful spot, where those from the surrounding towns who delight to view nature unadorned make their pilgrimage. These reservoirs, with the connecting goit, are from twenty-four to thirty-five miles distant from Liverpool, being nine (9) miles from end to end. They were constructed under the powers of an "Act of Parliament" passed in the year 1847, and derive their supplies of water from (principally), the rivers Douglas, the Yarrow, the Roddlesworth, and a number of smaller streams. The mean daily yield of water in the Rivington district on average of five years, from 1861 to 1865, amounted to 20,772,692 gallons, but only about half that quantity was availabe for use in Liverpool, namely, 10,542,800 gallons. The reservoirs are six (6) in number, covering an area of 549 acres, and when full contain 3,268,000,000 gallons of water. They are three and and half miles in length, and from fifty to seventy feet in depth.

The names and capacities of the reservoirs are as follows:—

(1.) The "Roddlesworth," upper reservoir, with an area of thirty-eight acres, and a depth of sixty-four (64) feet, capable of containing when full 180,000,000 gallons of water.

(2.) The "Roddlesworth" lower reservoir, covering 16 4-10 acres, of the depth of seventy-eight (78) feet, containing 79,600,000 gallons. These three reservoirs are connected with the others by means of a goit or canal, three and a half (3½) miles in length.

(3.) "Rake" reservoir, 13 3-10 acres, of the depth of seventy-eight (78) feet containing 79,600,000 gallons, also connected with the "goit."

(4.) The Anglezarke Reservoir, covering over 191 acres, of the depth of thirty-five (35) feet, and covering when full, 1,019,400,000 gallons of water.

(5.) The Chorley Reservoir, covering over 10 acres, of the depth of thirty-nine (39) feet, and containing 483,000,000 gallons.

(6.) The Rivington Reservoir, covering 275 acres, with a greatest depth of 40 feet, and capable of containing 1,841,000,000 gallons of water. The filter beds which lie at the base of the Rivington or delivery reservoir, cover 4 and 1-10th acres, and in ordinary work will filter 14,000,000 gallons of water daily.

The Corporation of Liverpool also obtained after powers to take an additional 2,000,000 gallons a day from the river Roddlesworth, and also constructed a kind of reserve reservoir, which is calculated to give an additional 5,000,000 gallons per day.

Having thus briefly sketched "The Lancashire Lakes," it may interest our readers to know, that though seemingly in a valley, the Rivington Waterworks, at their highest point, that is to say at the Upper Roddlesworth Reservoir are 619·8 feet above the level of the Old Dock Sill at Liverpool, while the filter beds, which appear to be really in a valley, are 382 feet above the Old Dock Sill. The distance from the Upper Roddlesworth Reservoir to Liverpool is thirty-four and a half (34½) miles. From the foot of the filter beds to Liverpool the water is conveyed through iron pipes for a distance of about twenty-four (24) miles. On the line of the pipes there is a reservoir for storing a quantity of water for immediate use at Eccleston, near Prescot, and there are also other smaller reservoirs around the city of the Liver. The greatest care is taken that the "water track," or pipe line, is kept in good order. Every morning a man leaves the water shed at Rivington, and walks along the pipe line till he meets another, who is responsible for another section, to whom he gives particulars of the rise or fall in the water level, and other information, and from section to section the news is conveyed to the Water Committee, each man in charge having given in his report.

The creation of these magnificent works had a most direful effect on the village of Horwich. Lee-lano was then almost entirely peopled with people who worked at the Horwich Vale Print Works, and the machine printers at that time commanded very high wages. Soon, however, it began to be alleged that the "bottom" water, which formed the compensation stream that flowed into their lodges was deleterious to the colours, and that it was a serious disadvantage to the works to use the water as sent down the stream. Law proceedings followed, and without further reference to this disputed point we will only say the result was that the "Vale Print Works" were stopped in October, 1860, and hundreds thrown out of employment, the lower part of Horwich being almost depopulated, and for a long time the large collection of buildings which formed the works were idle, and not till Mr. Cooke began the business of a paper manufacturer, which he still successfully carries on, did any sign of vitality exist. Messrs. Jolly and Jackson have now a portion of the same works, and for a long time Messrs. Rylands, of Manchester, also had a portion as a bleach works; but being denied a long lease (as we are informed) they removed their bleach works to Heapy, near Chorley. Thus, in benefiting the inhabitants of Liverpool, they of Horwich were called upon to suffer, and though perchance the beauty of the landscape has been increased, and the splendid water shed of the City on the Mersey has added another charm to the natural surroundings, yet this was at the expense of much suffering and inconvenience at the time.

CHAPTER XXXII.

BELOW we give the "MEMORANDUM OF AGREEMENT, made this twelfth day of May, one thousand eight hundred and fifty-two, between Christopher Shaw, of Rivington, in the County of Lancaster, gentleman, of one part, and the Mayor, Aldermen, and Burgesses of the Borough of Liverpool, in the County of Lancaster, of the other part. WITNESSETH that the said Christopher Shaw hereby consents and agrees that the said Mayor, Aldermen, and Burgesses may at any time hereafter, subject to the interests (if any) of the occupying tenants of the lands called The Gamsleys, and to the interests of the said Christopher Shaw as occupier of the estate called 'Hamers,' take possession of the lands called The Gamsleys, and such portion of the said estate called 'Hamers,' of the said Christopher Shaw, in Rivington, in the County of Lancaster, required by the said Mayor, Aldermen, and Burgesses, and which they have given notices to take for the purposes of the intended waterworks of the said Mayor, Aldermen, and Burgesses. And the said Mayor, Aldermen, and Burgesses will pay unto the said Christopher Shaw, interest after the rate of five pounds per centum per annum on the amount of the respective purchase, and compensation moneys which the said Christopher Shaw may be ultimately entitled to receive for the said lands and estate respectively. Such interest to be computed from the time or the respective times of the said Mayor, Aldermen, and Burgesses taking possession of the lands and estate respectively, or any part thereof, respectively, until the day or respective days of payment of the said respective purchase and consignment moneys. In witness whereof the said Mayor, Aldermen, and Burgesses to one part of these presents have hereunto affixed their common seal, and the said Christopher Shaw to the other part, hath herewith set his hand and seal the day and year above written."

THOMAS LITTLEDALE, Mayor.
(Corporation Seal.)

Then we pass on to the "folk lore of the district," and we may be permitted to glance at the lead mines at Anglezarke, and the wild expanse thereof, which perhaps in the near future may return valuable results to the explorers. Who that has visited its rural woods, entered its ravines, or perched themselves on its lovely knolls, and drank in some of those delightful inspirations that seem to nestle around Nature's grand story book, and has not been enraptured? If familiarity does not breed contempt, alas! too often it dims the mind and blunts the intellect, and these things of beauty are unnoticed. Once on a day Rivington was richer than now in her store of beauty that lay hid behind some projecting rock, or lost in the intricacies of her glens; but we will follow for a time a quondam Grammar School Master in his perambulations. Most of the reminiscences of Rivington, like many other places, have been handed down in the songs of her children during the occupation of "Buttercross," by John Brownlow. Some forty years ago a local rhymester said :—

There's old John o' Brownlow's, he lives at Buttercross,
He's a sad scolding wife and a child that is cross;
His looms are out of shot square, and his yarn it is crooked,
Which makes John ill tempered as he caures it nook.
　　　　　　　　　　　　　　　　　Derry down.

Let us now turn to the "Waterfall," which is situated at the head of Dean Valley. Formerly this was one of the prettiest sights to be seen even in beautiful Rivington; but the flow of water which gave such a picturesque charm to the fall has been in a great measure diverted from its original course by the tunnel made through the hill to convey the water to one of the reservoirs of the Liverpool Corporation. No spot was more visited during the summer months than this beautiful wood with its splendid fall, and the following descriptive lines will no doubt be read with interest :—

THE WATERFALL.

When little birds begin to mate,
　Gay parties come from town
To view the varied scenes around
　And places of renown,
A pleasant ride through country wide,
　With now and then a call,
Is sure to make the heart rejoice
　To see the waterfall.

A visit to the Black-a-Moor,
　Cigars, and beer, and grog,
The good old-fashioned days of yore,
　To set you all agog.

The fairy march begins to move,
  So buoyant, one and all;
Some wish to go to see the Pike,
  And some the waterfall.

Now, by the way, some wander wide,
  And 'mong the daisies play;
And some at rowly-powly romp,
  Among the new-made hay;
Some stray among the bushes, O!
  Then lounge beneath the wall—
O! ain't it nice to see the fun,
  And hear the waterfall?

And now they dance upon the lawn,
  And make the welkin ring;
A thousand times it has been
  That youth will have its fling.
A lady, starting up, exclaims,
  "I've left my parasol;
It's hanging on a little tree,
  Beside the waterfall!"

At last, the sun begins to fall,
  And all are homeward bound;
Sweet tales of never-ending love
  Are whispered round and round.
The morning breaks in golden rays,
  Bright scenes the soul enthral;
"O hadn't we a jolly spree
  Beside the waterfall."

In winter time the Valley of Dean presents as true a picture of desolation, as it does of beauty when " Sol as Monarch marches triumphantly through the air," and has been described in the following stanza:—

Sweet Valley of Dean, where the fairy is sleeping,
  In softest repose by the side of the stream,
Which falls from the rock where the siren is peeping,
  And lulls the soft echo who laughs in her dream.

Facing the village green, where on the occasion of the Black Boy Friendly Society's annual gathering the members meet to dance on the green sward, and enclosed within the walls of the present parsonage are the village stocks. These relics of a byegone period are in a good state of preservation, and below, enclosed in the grounds of the Ancient Grammar School, is the old " Sundial." A story is told of one of the schoolmasters, Rev. William Heaton, that he was passionately fond of star gazing, and upon one occasion an amourous youth who was waiting in " Love's blissful dream " the coming of his fair one, who chanced to be a servant at the house of the scholastacus, espied him coming out with his long instrument in his hand. Taking it for a weapon of a more destructive character, the youth sought shelter amongst the foliage of one of "the green yew trees." Raising the tube in the direction of the skies, he exclaimed with all the fervour of the star gazer, "Where is Orion?" The astonished youth imagining the instrument a blunderbuss, descended the tree and flew over the garden wall with a rush. The reverend star gazer was as much disconcerted as the youth to see "Orion" fall like a shooting star, and at once backed into the house, his meditations being disturbed for at least that night. As a fixture in this old schoolmaster's house, which now lie beneath the waters, was a grand old stairs of oak, which wound up to the top storey. This was obtained possession of by the late Rev. Thomas Sutcliffe, and is now a part of the interior fixings of the present parsonage. In the name "Street" which is given to the beautiful residence erected by the late Peter Martin, we have a very old name, and perhaps one that carries us back to the remote past when taken in juxtaposition with other mementos in the immediate neighbourhood.

CHAPTER XXXIII.

IMMEDIATELY in front of the street, the residence of the late Peter Martin, Esq., with the lake lying at its base, is one of those remarkable monuments of the past that ever form a source of controversy to the antiquarian, for here we have the remains of what must even now strike the eye as something out of the ordinary nature. To the most sceptical this portion of an embankment, or entrenchment, must rouse further investigation, and its marked delineation throws aside the theory that it is merely a long, natural mould of earth, heaped up in geometrical exactitude by some convulsion, some mysterious agency, the nature of which cannot be determined. Such an entrenchment, perhaps on more determined lines, has been allowed to be a defensive line for the archers of a former period as they discharged their arrows into the ranks of the enemy.

As we have before observed, the very name Rivington, which is common to all ancient documents, would imply the wandering class that dwelt under the shadow of its hills, or hid themselves within its intricate ravines. In fact, other names in the district are equally suggestive of its ancient character. On the borders of Anglezark is a deep ravine called "The Devil's Dyke," and it has been conjectured, with a good deal of probability, that the name is associated with the traditions of the district as having been constructed by the Ancient Druids to conceal their processions as they went to and fro in their religious ceremonies.

That Rivington and immediate districts have been suggestive of some of the discoveries which have marked the revolution that distinguishes the past from the present there can be no doubt. From scoriæ and fused nodules found in the bed of the streams, both above and below the village, as well as from the remains of furnaces found in the neighbourhood, gives a colouring to the suggestion that iron had been smelted from native ores in the no distant past, but all traces of workable ores of this metal are now lost. Within the memory of some now living in the uplands, and not far from the "Pike," remains of smelting furnaces were visible, with all the rubbish and refuse surrounding. There is no reason to doubt the statement, for the surroundings give every encouragement to the opinion, and even yet Rivington and neighbourhood may be a treasure trove when the "sun" of its neighbours has gone down. But these are the germs that may lead to further development, and those rolled blocks of a very coarse siliceous conglomerate lying on the surface around, which have no connection with any rocks, either superficial or quarried, in the neighbourhood, may be the "finger posts" to point the way. In the immediate neighbourhood lie the mines of Anglezark, worked at one time for lead ore. Yea, even to-day, a visit to "the lead mines" is spoken of by those who would ramble amongst the wilds and heather of Rivington's neighbour. From these mines the carbonate of baryta was first brought into notice among minerologists, under the name of Witherite, so called from Dr. Withering, the discoverer. In determining the position of these grand gathering grounds for their water supply, and fixing upon Rivington as a most probable and ready supply, the Corporation of Liverpool were guided by a principle which observation, atmospheric and hygrometic, pointed out as the most reliable. The surface of the country being very retentive of moisture, from the clay subsoil, as well as from its being mostly under green meadow and pasture, the atmosphere is soon brought to the saturated or dew point in any temperature, except when the wind is steadily from the east. Rain is, therefore, frequent, if not always severe. With westerly winds, and especially with those from the south-west, it is most frequent. In ordinary temperatures rain will fall at Rivington and neighbourhood from the same clouds that have passed over Liverpool, the presumption being that the electrical conditition of the hills inland is different from that of the clouds, as well as from the atmosphere around and over the hills being colder than the surface of the sea and land over which the clouds have previously been carried. To arrive at an approximate idea, relative say to Lancashire and other places, it has been pointed out that the amount of rainfall about London is not more than 25 inches, whilst the driest season that has been known in

Lancashire for many years, viz., that of 1865, gave a rainfall on the Lancashire hills, in the neighbourhood of Rivington, of 34·80 inches. During the seventeen years from 1849 to 1866, the average yearly rainfall on the Lancashire hills, in the neighbourhood of Rivington, was 45·70 inches, and in the season of 1861 the rainfall amounted to 61·70 inches. There can be no doubt that at the close of the last century Rivington bid fair to become more of a mercantile village than Horwich, though "Baines" has given to the latter the proud distinction of being the birth place of the important cotton industry which has raised the County Palatine to its present proud position. For even at "The Gouts," work was given out to the handloom weavers of Horwich and other places, and cottages were built having cellars underneath, in which "looms" were located, and, perhaps, earlier still than Horwich, did Rivington possess its bleaching croft or enclosure, where, much after the same manner as the modern domestic bleaches her clothes, were these long lines of cotton cloth stretched out on the grass, bleached long before M. Vallete brought chemical aid to bleaching, for in August, 1798, a man named John Eccles was charged with breaking into the bleaching grounds of Messrs. Tipping, at Horwich, and into the bleaching grounds of Mr. Entwistle, of Rivington, he being condemned to death, a verdict carried out in the September following.

CHAPTER XXXIV.

WE have before incidentally referred to that truly rural-looking structure called "Rivington Chapel," and, though not possessing a history chronologically equal to that of its near neighbour, yet there is sufficient in and around that quaint temple to stay the mind and rivet the eye, as from even the outward and visible signs the onlooker realises the fact that Rivington's history is more or less moulded by the silent ashes that now sleep within that enclosure, and that Rivington's past has been modified, and its future verily determined, by many who now sleep under its weeping shades, and whose record is protected by the overhanging willows.

We referred to the Rev. John Turner's military exploit, and from the Rev. Peter Walkden's diary we gather the information that the Rev. John Mayer was minister at Rivington Chapel in 1725, and under date of 1731, in the Northowram Register, we have the following :—" Mr. Samuel Astley, preacher at Rivington, was buried at Bolton, February 8th." But no succinct and proper account appears to hand of a place which has had important influence on the religious history of the surrounding districts, for there seems to be no doubt that "Lee Chapel," Horwich, is an offspring, born at a tempestuous period in the history of the Chapel at Rivington, when certain changes in the theological teachings were developed, and "Mourning the spread of Socinianism at Rivington" formed the Church at Horwich. But we are not concerned to enquire closely into certain changes developed out of events for which the period was famous. The Rev. B. Nightingale, who has devoted much research to this question, in an able article to the *Preston Guardian*, says :—"This is one of the earliest Lancashire Presbyterian Chapels that became Unitarian, and it has remained so ever since." By an indenture, dated January 20th, 1737, the following gifts were added to a former gift of Thomas Anderton of £100, and conveyed to trustees :—Lord Willoughby, £100; George Brownlow, late of Rivington, £50 by will ; Thos. Rivington, late of Anderton, yoeman, £20 by will ; James Worsley, late of Rivington, and widow, £15 ; Richard Kearshaw (Kershaw), late of Anglezark, £5 ; John Darbyshire, late of Rivington, £10 ; Thomas Johnson, late of Heath Charnock, £10 ; John Greenhalgh, late of Anderton, £5, and £5 saved out of interest; John Bradley, £50. One of the signatories was John Walker Street, Heath Charnock, clerk." From this it would appear probable that the two Walkers, father and son, ministered at Rivington.

The Rev. Samuel Bourn settled at Rivington in 1742, and from the fact that he was ordained by the Rev. Mr. Hardy, of Horwich, would seem to arise the collateral proof that there was sympathy and accordance in matters of doctrine and church government between the two churches. In 1703 a feeling of discontent had sprung up in various parts of the country, a discontent which was, to a large extent, fomented by the manner in which religious duties were performed by those called upon to minister in the temple, and also by that feeling of unrest which, like a hidden volcano, was ever threatening, a feeling engendered by the Reformation and outside the influence of all ecclesiastical authority. In this rural chapel were gathered those who were no longer able to drink of the waters of life at the Episcopal fountain, and whether Mr. Walker (previously referred to) was with them, or not, it is hard to determine. By a deed of gift of £100, dated January 16th, 1692, Thomas Anderton, yeoman, of Rivington, secured for the "Chappell" a rent charge of £5 10s., and in the *Notitia Cestriensis*, by Bishop Gastrell--Chetham Soc. Pub.—the following direct reference is made :— "£100 given formerly by Thos. Anderton, and £10 by his sister, now (about 1717) lost, supposed to have been applied by (the) Diss(enting) trustees to ye maint(enance) of yr teacher." The fact, says our author, is that Thos. Anderton was a Dissenter, and whatever may be the meaning of the word "Chappell" gave his money for Dissenting purposes. By an indenture, dated June 15th, 1704, John Andrew, of Little Lever, conveyed for 50s. received by him, land in Rivington for a chapel to the Right Hon. Hugh Willoughby, Baron of Parham, and others ; and the deed specified that "A chappell or oratory of four bays had been recently erected, intended to be a place for religious worship only, and for an assembly and meeting for a particular church or congregation of Protestants, dissenting from the Church of England, for the free exercise of Divine worship therein. Peaceable possession was given. Witnesses, Ra. Ainsworth, Jas. Brownlow, Peter Anderton." The Right Hon. Hugh had been distinguished for his Dissenting proclivities, and at Horwich Church he was equally demonstrative in his Nonconformist principles, and to such an extent was this shown that a letter was forwarded from the Rev. James Rothwell to Dr. Wroo, Warden of Manchester, complaining of his interference; the Ralph Ainsworth, whose name is first attached to the deed, and considering that he had signed the Cheshire Agreement of Presbyterian and Congregational Ministers, we may presume that the chapel was distinctly Presbyterian, a fact which is acknowledged to-day in the announcement of its annual sermon. And in Dr. Evan's list of Presbyterians and Independents—1717-1729—Rivington is included in the list, and is returned as capable of accommodating 329 persons, and the pastor, the Rev. John Turner. The date of the Rev. W. Gaskell's appointment is not known, but it is certain that he ministered here in 1770, for we find his signature in the baptismal registers, and as they date from this period no determined guide can be found. The Rev. Thomas Rawlins followed in 1778. He was the son of the Rev. John Rawlins, some time minister at Hoghton Tower. He married Margaret Pilkington, of the Pilkington family of Rivington. The Rev. Nathaniel Hibbert first signed the register, says our author, as minister at Rivington, in 1784. He died on the 30th June, 1819, at the age of 57 years, and was buried in the chapel graveyard. His tombstone records that he was minister 36 years. The Rev. James Taylor came next, settling in Rivington in 1820. He removed to Dob-lane Chapel in 1833, and died in 1862. His daughter has contributed some beautiful pieces of statuary to Peel Park Art Gallery, and gave a painted window to Dob-lane Chapel. She has also published a volume of poems, and signs her name as "Kate Taylor Robinson." The Rev. John Jenkins appeared as a supply during the years 1832-4, but was not the regular minister. Repeated changes now follow each other. The Rev. G. H Wells came in 1833, and resigned 1837, the Rev. W. Rowlinson from 1837 to 1840; and the Rev. E. R Dimmock followed, with a one year's stay.

CHAPTER XXXV.

THE Rev. C. W. Robberds, a Manchester College student, son of the Rev. John Gooch Robberds, of Cross-street, Manchester, and, through his mother, descended from the Rev. John Turner, already referred to, was at Rivington from 1812-3. He was followed in 1843 by the Rev. Cubit Boardman Hubbard. He was born at Wacton Hall, Norfolk, on the 21st of April, 1779, and was educated at Homerton, and died on the 11th of April, 1854. He was buried in the chapel yard, and his tombstone gives the above particulars. The Rev. J. S. Gilbert is well-known by even those of the present generation. Little in stature, but withal possessed of a most active mind, his sermons were those of the deep thinker. Broad in his sympathies, fearless in the exposition of his opinions, which were always conveyed in language of the most attractive style, almost poetic in their ideal, his discourses gave subject for thought; while in their attractiveness they commanded the ready attention of the listener. He, too, is buried within that beautiful rural enclosure, and his tombstone records that he was "born at Plymouth May 10th, 1816," and that for 25 years he was a faithful minister of this chapel. He died at Altrincham, November 20th, 1885, and was "an earnest student, a conscientious teacher, and a constant friend." Of the present Rev. Samuel Thompson little need be said, as his character and doings, his energy, and genial disposition are well-known and acknowledged beyond the rural district where he labours. He was trained at Owen's and the Home Missionary Colleges, and entered into his charge at Rivington in 1881. There is a neat and commodious Schoolroom in close contiguity to the chapel, built by public subscription and opened by the well-known George Dawson, of Birmingham. The Library in connection with this Chapel was formerly a most noted one throughout the district, and any works of advanced thought, no matter to what particular theological or other school they might belong, were sure to find a resting place here; and youths in the surrounding district could command works from this well-managed Library, which were denied them elsewhere. Its annual sermon commanded the keenest interest, and "Rivington Presbyterian Chapel" was the centre to which vehicles and pedestrians alike tended. Some of the "lights" of the School have been found on such occasions within his pulpit, men who have left their mark behind them, and whose fearless exposition of their opinions have made them a name "beyond the age." The Chapel has its Manse or parsonage which is situated a little higher than the Chapel—Pikewards. This Manse was built at the close of the last century, and land for the same was conveyed by deed dated July 31st, 1786, from Robert Andrews, Esq., of Rivington Hall, to Abram Crompton and others. The Library was the offspring of the efforts of the Rev. James Taylor about the year 1821, and the care and attention bestowed upon its inception has been manifested and sustained to the present.

Dr. Martineau, the well-known author, was formerly an occasional visitor at Rivington, its rural charms having an interest for him; and he thus describes a visit paid here when the "Methodist" looked upon Rivington as a fitting place for their attentions. Choosing the "green" in the immediate vicinity of the chapel and the vicarage, these invasions roused somewhat the ire of the then ecclesiastical chief of the church. "We remember," says Dr. Martineau, "what occurred in a village situated amongst the hills of one of our northern dioceses. On a fine summer evening we had gone, at the close of the afternoon service, for a stroll through the field overlooking the valley. When we had walked half a mile or so, an extraordinary din arose from the direction of the village, sounding like nothing human or instrumental, larynx, catgut, or brass, though occasionally mingled with an undeniable note from some shouting stentor. It was evident through the trees, that a crowd was collected on the village green, and not less so, that a farmer and his wife, who were looking on from a stile hard by, understood the scene below. On asking what all the hubbub was about, we were told by the good woman, 'It's all our parson, that's banging out the Methody wi' t' tae booard.' Being curious in ecclesiastical researches, we hastened down the hill, in spite of the repulsion of increasing noise. On one side of the green was a deal table, from which a field preacher was holding forth with passionate, but fruitless energy ; for, on the other side, and at the back of the crowd, was the parochial man of God, who had issued from his parsonage, armed with its largest tea-tray and the hall door key, and was battering the japan in the service of orthodoxy. No military music could more effectually neutralise the shrieks of battle. The more the Evangelist bellowed, the faster went the parish gong. It was impossible to confute the drum ecclesiastic, and the Methody's brass was fairly beaten out of the field by the Churchman's tin."

Between the Episcopal Church and the Quondam Presbyterian Chapel there has always existed the greatest harmony and good feeling, and Rivington in its religious characteristics has shown an example which would develope nobler traits, were they more acted upon in the Church at large. Rivington Chapel, both in its associations and traditions, is inseparably connected with Rivington's history ; yea, and much of the history of Lancashire's busy centres are re-echoed from its silent grave yard. Darbyshire, Bolton's first Mayor, Harwoods of Salford and Manchester, and others who have left their footprints on the sands of time, await here, the trumpet's sound, when time shall be no more, and earth's record cease, to merge into that Eternal One, which even the mind cannot grasp.

The baptismal registers point to the fact how much of interest was centred in this rural Chapel in the past, by the records they give from Blackrod, Horwich, and other outside districts. When the Chapel Library Scheme was broached one of its readiest supporters was the Rev. James Jackson, who was incumbent of the church at the time, and this rev. cleric was not only noted for his eccentricity, but also for the very agreeable manner in which he performed his functions. But rural Rivington was not the place where the cleric needed to fear the over critical eye. It was enough that he read the prayers on a Sunday, buried their dead, and baptised their children ; and if perchance he was seen in the kitchen at the Black Boy, and smoked his long pipe with farmer Smithels, and had his glass of stout while he conversed with the village blacksmith ; was a carver at their club day feast, and preached to them ere they dined, this did not dim his spiritual calling or deduct from the sanctity of his office. If he was a clergyman he was none the less a man, and in the unity of the two he drew forth the love and esteem of his rural parishioners What more could even a clergyman do ? and, perhaps, in this commingling he served his Master better than those whose demeanour is only the outward reading of the inward thought —"Stand back, I am holier than thou." This reciprocal feeling was, until lately, illustrated in the closing of the church or the chapel when the anniversary sermons, took place, and who will say that Rivington was any the worse for this mutual sympathy. Rivington Presbyterian Chapel was one of the first to become Unitarian, and has so remained. Rivington, however, is secure, for a time at least, for accommodation at religious worship for the 330 of a population given in 1881, and little change, we opine, followed in 1891.

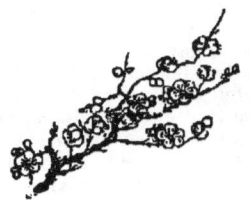

CHAPTER XXXVI.

IN bringing to a close our contribution to local history, we beg to acknowledge our obligations to our friends for their kind aid, and our indebtedness to many who have made the County Palantine their special study ; and though we cannot lift the veil of the future, or look beyond the present, yet we opine that, though protected from the invasion of the manufacturer, we cannot expect Rivington to wear its rural look, or its sunny shades to be left for the sport of the wild bee, and its uplands a picture where nature reigns supreme. Year by year its attractive spots are more widely known, its lanes busier with the sound of wheels, and its shaded groves re-echo more and more the human voice divine. Its sudden nooks are more explored, its rippling streams and its mountain gushes more recognised, and year by year the hand of the vandal is making its woods more barren, its gems of Nature's own floriculture are decreasing, and herbs for the use of man are conveyed from their native soil to wither and die in uncongenial spots. Its ferns are ruthlessly torn from the virgin soil, and weep and die in their new abode. How long this will be permitted we know not, but to destroy, even in their efforts to possess a fragment of rural beauty, is none the less a crime. Rivington has more than sufficiently been robbed of her birthright in the educational schemes of the past, without suffering in her outward aspect, and in referring to her educational facilities we are reminded of the fact that to-day Rivington is more protected in having within her borders gentlemen who by their position and influence can well watch over the interest of the inhabitants. For even the action of the governors of its school was not permitted to go unchallenged, as the following reply of the ex-governors to the statement made by Walton Ainsworth, as spokesman for the present governors, will show :—

"Our attention has been called to a statement recently published and circulated amongst members of Parliament, and which we beg to submit is founded on an erroneous impression of facts and circumstances connected with the scheme now laid before Parliament. In the first place we beg to call attention to the statement ' that the school will be deprived of much property, and the chapel will lose the benefit of the use of the school, without any equivalent to either.' In reply to this we beg to state that there is a very large equivalent provided for this surrender of property, although this surrender is made for purposes solely educational, and for the general benefit of the district, Rivington included. 'Shaw's Charity Trustees' expressly stipulate to devote half their entire income towards the maintenance of the elementary schools to be established in Rivington and Heath Charnock, which contribution or equivalent is worth fully £180 a year at present, with a fair prospect of being very largely increased on the opening out of the coal well known to be under the land belonging to the aforesaid Shaw's Charity. This equivalent will, if the scheme be carried out, enable the new governing body to reduce the scale of fees to a very low rate indeed, or enable it to admit a considerable number of poor children entirely free of charge, if that mode be thought desirable. Then as to the church using the room for a Sunday school, not one person, Churchman or Dissenter, who is likely to be elected a Governor, but who has already given a promise to continue the same privilege that has hitherto been conceded by courtesy, not by absolute right, to the Church at Rivington."

" How much like a satire, when we remember, as shown in these pages, to whom Rivington owes its school and its privileges, does the above sentence read. Then, as to the statement that the New School is to be erected in Anderton, where there is no church or place of worship, except a Roman Catholic Church, we have to say that already provision is made, with the approval of the Ecclesiastical Commissioners to build, out of the surplus revenues of Standish Parish, and with the consent of the present Rector, a church fully adequate to all the wants of the locality, and in a situation conveniently near the proposed site of the new school. Then, as to the inhabitants of the several townships being opposed ' to the removal of the school out of Rivington,' that remark only applies to those parties *who will not* understand the plain fact that no one wants to remove the school out of Rivington, there being ample provisions made for its retention there, in a greatly enlarged and improved form. With regard to the so-called public meeting held in Rivington on the 21st January, the figures given are greatly exaggerated one way, and under stated the other ; and the less said about the meeting the better for those concerned in promoting it and managing its proceedings."

" We have now to call special attention to the statement as to the meeting of the 12th May, 1873, when it states that only one person was in favour of the amalgamation of the two schools, and that no one seconded his amendment to that effect. In the first place, the date of this occurrence is inaccurate ; but then, why does not Mr. Walton Ainsworth state what he knows to be true ? That before and after this date several meetings were held, at which perfectly unanimous resolutions were carried in favour of the amalgamation, and that Mr. Ainsworth was as much in favour of it as anyone, and formed one of a deputation that went up to London to discuss some of the details of the measure, on the 30th July, 1873, and which said deputation did there and then come to a unanimous decision in favour of the Scheme as now presented to Parliament. And why, again, does not Mr. Ainsworth state also the following fact, that in October, 1873, the Governors of Rivington School, through their solicitor, Mr. Rushton, wrote a formal letter to the Endowed School Commission, expressly stating their approval, and which letter can now be seen at the Office of the Endowed School Commission ? And why does not Mr. Ainsworth also state the fact that some time after the before-mentioned occurrences—and after the Governors had repeatedly given their unanimous assent to all the provisions of the scheme—he (Mr. Walton Ainsworth) himself, at a meeting specially called by request of the Endowed School Commission, did propose and carry the resolution by which the two co-optative Governors now mentioned in the Scheme were appointed ? Why all these important facts are withheld, and why two Governors have recently resigned their governorships ought to be explained. But as to the correctness of this statement we pledge ourselves, and undertake to prove it by a reference to the Minute Books of the School, and as ex-Governors of Rivington School beg respectfully to attach our names—Thomas Middleton, Adam Mason."

Notwithstanding this bickering, this straining at a gnat and swallowing a camel, the fact is ever patent to those who have opportunity to study the question, that the school has been estranged from its original purpose, that the will and wish of its "pious founder" has been frustrated and sacrificed, that it is now removed out of the list of "free scholes" which the "learned prelate, James Pilkington, Bishopp of Duresme," intended it ever to be; that the "Royal Grant" and "Letters Patent" of the 13th of May, in the 8th year of Elizabeth's reign, are thrown to the winds; that the "Free Grammar School of Queen Elizabeth, in Rovington, *alias* Rivington," has been diverted from its object, and its name a misnomer; and instead of being for the benefit of the "poore" in the districts interested, it has virtually become a "college" where the rich and opulent alone can gather. For this, perhaps, those most interested are to blame, and in this respect Blackrod and Rivington must equally bear their share and though succeeding generations may question the right of sequestration, to disturb an institution may not prove a policy which wisdom would dictate, yet "rights and privileges" neglected are not always lost, and the *Vox Populi Vox Dei* may again prove that the "Voice of the people is the voice of God."

The Rivington and Blackrod Grammar School will ere the year 1892 closes, have a beautiful school chapel opened on the Rivington side of the present building which is being erected at the cost of Mr. Marshall, brewer, Bolton. The architect is Mr. R. K. Freeman, of Bolton, whose object has evidently been to keep in view harmony of design. The original estimate of £1,100 has already been exceeded, and no doubt will be still further increased. The boys will then be enabled to avail themselves of their devotional duties within their own domain, and the connecting link which binds the past to the present will at least have a religious association in keeping with the memoirs of those bye-gone sons— Pilkington and Vaux—who intended so much for their native hamlets, however much such intention may have suffered in more modern administration.

THE END.

APPENDIX.

RIVINGTON AND BLACKROD UNITED SCHOOLS.

Subjoined is a copy of the New Scheme in this matter in the form in which it was on the 10th November, 1892, approved by the Lord President, and, on the 30th January, 1893, by Her Majesty in Council:—

No. 730.

E
45,881.

CHARITY COMMISSION.

County—LANCASTER.
Parish—BOLTON-LE-MOORS.
Township—RIVINGTON.
Endowment—Rivington and Blackrod United Schools.

In the Matter of the Foundation known as the RIVINGTON and BLACKROD UNITED SCHOOLS, in the township of Rivington, in the parish of Bolton-le-Moors, in the county of Lancaster; and

In the Matter of the Endowed Schools Act, 1869, and Amending Acts.

SCHEME FOR THE ADMINISTRATION OF THE ABOVE-MENTIONED FOUNDATION.

1.—This Foundation and its endowment, set out or referred to in the Schedule hereto, shall henceforth be administered under this Scheme, under the name of Rivington and Blackrod Grammar School, hereinafter and in the Schedule hereto called the Foundation.

2.—Subject as herein provided, the Foundation shall be administered by a Governing Body, hereinafter called the Governors, consisting of seventeen competent persons duly qualified to discharge the duties of the office, thirteen to be called Representative Governors, and four to be called Coöptative Governors.

3.—The Representative Governors shall, except as herein provided, be appointed by the following electing bodies respectively in the following proportions, that is to say :—

    One by the Council of St. John's College in the University of Cambridge ;
    One by the County Council of the County Palatine of Lancaster ;
    One by the Council of the Victoria University ;
    Two by the ratepayers of the townships or places of Rivington, Anglezarke, and Sharples Higher End ;
    Two by the ratepayers of the townships of Heath Charnock and Anderton ;
    Two by the Local Board of Horwich ;
    One by the Local Board of Adlington ; and
    Three by the Local Board of Blackrod.

The persons in office at the date of this Scheme as Nominated or Representative Governors of the Foundation shall remain in office as Representative Governors under this Scheme, each for the remainder of the term for which he was appointed, and in other respects shall be counted, as to the Governor nominated by the Master and Seniors of St. John's College aforesaid as if he had been appointed under this Scheme by the Council of the same College, and as to the Governors elected by any of the other above-named electing bodies, as if they had been appointed under this Scheme each by the electing body by which he was elected. Each appointment by an electing body shall be made at a meeting thereof convened and held as nearly as may be in accordance with the ordinary rules or practice, if any, of such body, or in case of need or doubt in accordance with rules to be made or approved by the Charity Commissioners for England and Wales. The Representative Governors hereafter to be appointed shall be appointed to office each for the term of five years reckoned from the date of his appointment. Subject as aforesaid, the first Representative Governors shall be appointed as soon as conveniently may be after the date of this Scheme. The Chairman or other presiding officer of each meeting at which the appointment of any Representative Governors or Governor shall be made shall forthwith cause the names or name of the persons or person so appointed to be notified to the Chairman of the Governors or their clerk, if any, or other agent. Subject as aforesaid, any appointment of a Representative Governor not made as aforesaid within six calendar months from the date of this Scheme, or of the notice hereinafter prescribed of a vacancy, as the case may be, shall for that turn be made by the then existing Governors.

4.—The persons in office at the date of this Scheme as Coöptative Governors of the Foundation shall remain in office as Coöptative Governors under this Scheme, each for the remainder only of the term for which he was appointed. The Coöptative Governors hereafter to be appointed shall be appointed, each for the term of eight years, by the general body of Governors at a special meeting.

5.—Any Governor who shall become bankrupt or incapacitated to act, or shall notify in writing to the Governors his wish to resign, or shall for the space of two consecutive years omit to attend any meeting, shall thereupon vacate the office of Governor ; and the Governors shall cause an entry to be made in their minute book of every vacancy caused as aforesaid or by the death or the expiration of the term of office of any Governor ; and as soon as conveniently may be after any vacancy a new Governor shall be appointed by the body entitled as aforesaid to make such appointment. Any Governor may be re-appointed. Notice of every vacancy of the office of Representative Governor shall be given as soon as conveniently may be by or under the direction of the Governors to the proper electing body or the clerk, if any, or other agent of such body.

6.—Religious opinions, or attendance or non-attendance at any particular form of religious worship, shall not in any way affect the qualification of any person for being a Governor under this Scheme.

7.—Every Governor shall, at or before the first meeting which he attends upon his first or any subsequent entry into office, sign a memorandum declaring his acceptance of the office of Governor, and his willingness to act in the trusts of this Scheme, and until he has signed such a memorandum shall not be entitled to act as a Governor.

8.—The Governors shall hold their meetings in some convenient place in Rivington or elsewhere, and shall hold at least two ordinary meetings in each year. Notice in writing of each ordinary meeting shall be delivered or sent by post to each Governor by the clerk, if any, or by some other person acting under the direction of the Governors at least seven days before such meeting.

9.—The Chairman or any two Governors may at any time summon a special meeting for any cause that seems to him or them sufficient. All special meetings shall be convened, by or under the direction of the person or persons summoning the meeting, by notice in writing delivered or sent by post to each Governor specifying the object of the meeting. And it shall be the duty of the clerk, if any, to give such notice when required by the Chairman or by any two Governors.

10.—The Governors shall at their first ordinary meeting in each year elect one of their number to be Chairman of their meetings for such year. They shall make regulations for supplying his place in case of his death, resignation, or absence. The Chairman shall always be re-eligible.

11.—There shall be a quorum when six Governors are present at a meeting. Every question at a meeting, except as herein provided, shall be determined by the majority of the Governors present and voting on the question, and in case of equality of votes the Chairman shall have a second or casting vote. Any resolution of the Governors may be rescinded or varied at a special meeting held after not less than seven days' notice.

12.—If at the time appointed for a meeting a sufficient number of Governors to form a quorum are not present, or if at any meeting the business is not completed, the Governors present may adjourn the meeting to a day and time, of which, if the meeting is adjourned for more than two days, notice shall forthwith be delivered or sent by post to each Governor.

13.—A minute book shall be provided and kept by the Governors, and minutes of the entry into office of every new Governor, and of all proceedings of the Governors, shall be entered in such minute book.

14.—The Governors shall make out and render to the Charity Commissioners, such accounts as shall be required by such Commissioners, and shall also, on rendering accounts for any year to such Commissioners, exhibit for public inspection in some convenient place in Rivington copies of the accounts so rendered for such year, giving due public notice where and when the same may be seen, and shall at all reasonable times allow the accounts so rendered for any year or years to be inspected, and copies thereof or extracts therefrom to be made, by all persons applying for the purpose.

15.—The Governors may from time to time make such arrangements as they may find most fitting for the custody of all deeds and other documents belonging to the Foundation, for deposit of money, for the drawing of cheques, and for the appointment of a clerk or of any necessary agents for their assistance in the conduct of the business of the Foundation at such reasonable salaries or scale of remuneration as shall be approved by the Charity Commissioners, but no Governor acting as such clerk or agent shall receive any salary or remuneration.

16.—The freehold and leasehold land and hereditaments belonging to the Foundation are hereby vested in the Official Trustee of Charity Lands and his successors for all the estate and interest of the Foundation therein. All stock, shares, funds, and securities belonging to the Foundation shall be forthwith transferred under the authority of an Order of the Charity Commissioners into the name of the Official Trustees of Charitable Funds. The Governors and all other persons capable of being bound by this Scheme shall, unless the Charity Commissioners otherwise order, do all such acts as may be necessary in order to vest in the Official Trustee of Charity Lands all the freehold and leasehold land and hereditaments, and to transfer to the Official Trustees of Charitable Funds all the stocks, shares, funds, and securities which may hereafter belong to the Foundation.

17.—The property of the Foundation not occupied for the purposes thereof shall be let or otherwise managed by the Governors, or by their agents acting under their orders according to the general law applicable to the management of property by trustees of charitable foundations. All payments for rates, taxes, repairs, and insurance of, or in respect of, any such property occupied for the purposes of the Foundation shall, so far as not otherwise provided for, be made out of the income of the Foundation.

18.—Any money arising from the sale of timber or from any mines or minerals on the estates of the Foundation shall be treated as capital, and shall be invested in the name of the Official Trustees of Charitable Funds under the direction of the Charity Commissioners, except in any special cases in which the Governors may be authorised by such Commissioners to deal otherwise with such money or any part thereof.

19.—The Governors for the time being, if a quorum is formed, may act for all the purposes of this Scheme, although the number of Governors as herein-before constituted is not full.

20.—So far as may be not inconsistent with anything contained in the Endowed Schools Act, 1869, and Amending Acts, the School may be carried on as heretofore until the end of the school term, if any, current at the date of this Scheme, or until such other time as may, with the approval of the Charity Commissioners, be fixed by the Governors.

21.—The present Head Master shall, if willing, take and hold the office of Head Master of the school under this Scheme.

22.—Any holder of a Scholarship or Exhibition awarded on or before the 31st day of December, 1891, shall be entitled to hold his Scholarship or Exhibition as if this Scheme had not been made.

23.—The Governors shall take all proper measures for carrying the provisions of this Scheme into effect as soon as practicable.

THE SCHOOL.

24.—The School of the Foundation shall be a School for boys, and shall be maintained in or near the township of Rivington in the present school buildings or in other suitable buildings hereafter to be provided for the purpose by the Governors. It shall be for day scholars and for boarders.

25.—There shall be a Head Master of the School. He shall be a member of the Church of England and a graduate of some University in the British Empire, or have such other qualification or certificate or other test of his attainments as may be fixed from time to time by any regulation of the Governors approved by the Charity Commissioners. Every Head Master hereafter to be appointed shall be appointed by the Governors at a special meeting to be held as soon as conveniently may be after a vacancy or after notice of an intended vacancy. In order to get the best candidates, the Governors, before making any appointment, shall give public notice of the vacancy and invite applicants for the office by advertisements in newspapers, or by such other means as they may judge best calculated to secure the object.

26.—The Governors may at pleasure dismiss the Head Master without assigning cause, after six calendar months' written notice, given to him in pursuance of a resolution passed at two special meetings held at an interval of not less than fourteen days, such resolution being affirmed at each meeting by not less than two thirds of the Governors present and voting on the question.

27.—The Governors, for what in their opinion is urgent cause, may by a resolution passed at a special meeting and affirmed by not less than two thirds of the whole number of Governors for the time being declare that the Head Master ought to be dismissed from his office, as in this clause provided, and in that case they may appoint a second special meeting to be held not less than a week after the first, and may, by a like resolution, passed at such second meeting, and affirmed by not less than two thirds of the whole number of Governors for the time being, thereupon absolutely and finally dismiss him. And if at the first of such meetings the Governors think fit at once to suspend the Head Master from his office until the second of such meetings, they may so suspend him by a resolution affirmed by not less than two thirds of the whole number of Governors for the time being. Full notice and opportunity of defence at both such meetings shall be given to the Head Master.

28.— Every Head Master before taking office under this Scheme shall sign a declaration, to be entered in the minute book of the Governors, to the following effect :—

"I, , declare that I will always to the
"best of my ability discharge the duties of Head
"Master of the Rivington and Blackrod Grammar
"School during my tenure of the office, and that if I
"am removed therefrom, I will thereupon acquiesce
"in such removal, and relinquish all claim to the
"mastership and its future emoluments, and deliver
"up to the Governors, or, as they direct, possession
"of all the property of the School then in my pos-
"session or occupation."

29.—The Head Master shall dwell in the residence, if any, assigned for him. The occupation and use of such residence, and of any other property of the Foundation occupied by him as Head Master, shall be had by him in respect of his official character and duties, and not as tenant, and if he is removed from his office, he shall deliver up possession of such residence and other property to the Governors, or as they direct. He shall not, except with the permission of the Governors, permit any person not being a member of his family to occupy such residence or any part thereof.

30.—The Head Master shall give his personal attention to the duties of the School, and shall not hold any benefice having the cure of souls, or undertake any office or employment interfering with the proper performance of his duties as Head Master.

31.—No Head Master or Assistant Master of the School shall be a Governor.

32.—No Head Master or Assistant Master shall receive or demand from any boy in the School, or from any person whomsoever on behalf of any such boy, any gratuity, fee, or payment, except such as are prescribed or authorised by or under this Scheme.

33.—Within the limits fixed by this Scheme, the Governors shall prescribe the general subjects of instruction, the relative prominence and value to be assigned to each group of subjects, the arrangements respecting the school terms, vacations, and holidays, the payments of day scholars, and the number and payments of boarders. They shall take general supervision of the sanitary condition of the school buildings and arrangements. They shall fix the number of Assistant Masters to be employed. They shall every year fix the amount which they think proper to be paid out of the income of the Foundation for the purpose of maintaining Assistant Masters and providing and maintaining a proper school plant or apparatus.

34.—Before making any regulations under the last foregoing clause, the Governors shall consult the Head Master in such a manner as to give him full opportunity for the expression of his views. The Head Master may also from time to time submit proposals to the Governors for making or altering regulations concerning any matter within the province of the Governors. The Governors shall fully consider any such expression of views or proposals, and shall decide upon them.

35.—Subject to any rules prescribed by or under the authority of this Scheme, the Head Master shall have under his control the choice of books, the method of teaching, the arrangement of classes and school hours, and generally the whole internal organisation, management, and dicipline of the School, including the power of expelling boys from the School or suspending them from attendance thereat for any adequate cause to be judged of by him, but on expelling or suspending any boy he shall forthwith report the case to the Governors.

36.—The Head Master shall have the sole power of appointing, and may at pleasure dismiss all Assistant Masters in the School, and shall determine, subject to the approval of the Governors, in what proportions the sum fixed by the Governors for the maintenance of Assistant Masters and school plant and apparatus shall be divided among the various persons and objects for which it is fixed in the aggregate, and the Governors shall pay the same accordingly, either through the hands of the Head Master or directly as they think best.

37.—The Head Master shall receive a fixed yearly stipend of 150*l*. He shall also receive a capitation payment calculated on such a scale, uniform or graduated, as may be fixed from time to time by the Governors, at the rate of not less than 2*l*. nor more than 5*l*. a year for each boy in the School. He shall also receive a further sum of not less than 1*l*. nor more than 2*l*. yearly for each boarder in a hostel.

38.—All boys, including boarders, except as herein provided, shall pay entrance and tuition fees to be fixed from time to time by the Governors, such entrance fees being not more than 1*l*. for any boy, and such tuition fees being at the rate of not less than 5*l*. nor more than 10*l*. a year for any boy. No difference in respect of entrance or tuition fees shall be made between any scholars on account of place of birth or residence, or of their being or not being boarders. The payments of boarders, apart from the entrance and tuition fees, shall be at the rate of not more than 35*l*. a year for any boy under the age of sixteen years, nor more than 45*l*. a year for any other boy. No extra or additional payment of any kind shall be allowed without the sanction of the Governors, and the written consent of the parent, or person occupying the place of parent, of the scholar concerned. All payments for entrance and tuition fees shall be made in advance to the Head Master, or to such other person as the Governors shall from time to time fix, and shall be accounted for by the person receiving them to the Governors, and be treated by them as part of the general income of the Foundation.

39.—No boy shall be admitted to the School under the age of eight years. No boy shall remain in the School after the age of seventeen years, or if he attains that age during a school term, then after the end of such term, except with the permission of the Governors, which in special cases may be given until the age of eighteen years upon the written recommendation of the Head Master.

40.—Subject to the provisions established by or under the authority of this Scheme, the School and all its advantages shall be open to all boys of good character and sufficient health who are residing with their parents, guardians, or near relations within degrees to be fixed by the Governors, or are boarding under regulations made by the Governors, either in a hostel of the Foundation or in the house of any Master. No boy not so residing or boarding shall be admitted to the School without the special permission of the Governors.

41.—Applications for admission to the School shall be made to the Head Master, or to some person appointed by the Governors, according to a form to be approved by them, and delivered to all applicants.

42.—The Head Master or some person appointed by the Governors shall keep a register of applications for admission, showing the date of every application and of the admission, withdrawal, or rejection of the applicant, and the cause of any rejection, and the age of each applicant.

43.—Every applicant for admission shall be examined by or under the direction of the Head Master. The Head Master shall appoint convenient times for that purpose, and give reasonable notice to the parents or next friends of the boy to be so examined. No boy shall be admitted to the School except after undergoing such examination and being found fit for admission. Those who are so found fit shall, if there is room for them, be admitted in order according to the dates of their application. The examination for admission shall be graduated according to the age of the boy, and shall be regulated in other particulars from time to time by or under the direction of the Governors, but it shall never fall below the following standard, that is to say :—

Reading ;
Writing from dictation ;
Sums in the first four simple rules of Arithmetic, with the Multiplication Table.

44.—Subject to the provisions of this Scheme, religious instruction in accordance with the doctrines of the Church of England shall be given in the

School. Instruction shall also be given in the School in the following subjects :—
> Reading, Writing, and Arithmetic ;
> Geography and History ;
> English Grammar, Composition, and Literature ;
> Mathematics ;
> Latin ;
> At least one modern Foreign European Language ;
> Natural Science ;
> Drawing, Drill, and Vocal Music.

Subject to the provisions of this Scheme, the course of instruction shall be according to the classification and arrangements made by the Head Master.

45.—There shall be once in every year an examination of the scholars. The Examiner or Examiners shall, except as herein provided, be appointed or approved by the Governors, but otherwise unconnected with the School. In any year the Charity Commissioners may by an Order direct that the Examiner or Examiners for that year shall be appointed in any other manner, and the examination shall for that year be held in the manner so directed. The day of examination shall be fixed by the Governors after consulting the Head Master. The cost of the examination shall be paid by the Governors out of the income of the Foundation. The Examiner or Examiners shall report in writing to the Governors on the proficiency of the scholars and on the condition of the School as regards instruction and discipline, as shown by the result of the examination. The Governors shall send a copy of the report to the Head Master and to the Charity Commissioners.

46.—The Head Master shall make a report in writing to the Governors yearly at such time as they shall direct on the general condition and progress of the School, and on any special occurrences during the year. He may also mention the names of any boys who, in his judgment, are worthy of reward or distinction, having regard both to proficiency and conduct.

47.—The Governors may award prizes of books or other suitable rewards as marks of distinction to any boys mentioned as worthy of reward or distinction by the Head Master or by the Examiner or Examiners.

48.—Not less than ten Scholarships, to be called Foundation Scholarships, in the form of total exemptions from the payment of tuition fees, shall be maintained in the School. These Scholarships shall be awarded to boys who are and have for not less than two years been scholars in any of the Public Elementary Schools in the said eight townships or places of Rivington, Anglezarke, Sharples Higher End, Heath Charnock, Anderton, Horwich, Adlington, and Blackrod. The Governors shall make such arrangements for the elections to these Scholarships as seem to them best adapted to secure the double object of attracting good scholars to the School of this Foundation, and advancing education at the said Public Elementary Schools.

49.—Other Scholarships in the form of exemptions, total or partial, from the payment of tuition fees may, if the income of the Foundation will allow, be maintained in the School at the rate of not more than one such other Scholarship for every ten boys in the School.

50.—The Governors may, during a period of five years from the date of this Scheme, and afterwards shall maintain exhibitions, each of a yearly value of not more than £40, tenable for three years at any institution for higher education approved by the Governors and to be awarded one or more in each year to boys who then are and have not for less than two years been in the School.

51.—The Scholarships and Exhibitions shall be established in such manner and order as to secure as nearly as may be a regular rotation of award, and, subject as herein provided, shall be awarded and held under such regulations and conditions as the Governors think fit. Every Scholarship and Exhibition shall be given as the reward of merit on the result of such examination as the Governors think fit, and shall, except as herein provided, be freely and openly competed for, and shall be tenable only for the purposes of education. Any Scholarship or Exhibition for which there shall be no duly qualified candidate, who on examination shall be adjudged worthy to take it, shall for that turn not be awarded.

52.—If the holder of a Scholarship or Exhibition shall, in the judgment of the Governors, be guilty of serious misconduct or idleness, or fail to maintain a reasonable standard of proficiency, or wilfully cease to pursue his education, the Governors may deprive him of the Scholarship or Exhibition, and for this purpose, in the case of an Exhibition may act on the report of the proper authorities of the Institution at which the Exhibition is held, or on such other evidence as the Governors think sufficient. Under this clause the decision of the Governors shall be final in each case.

GENERAL.

53.—The parent or guardian of, or person liable to maintain or having the actual custody of, any scholar attending the School as a day scholar may claim by notice in writing addressed to the Head Master the exemption of such scholar from attending prayer or religious worship, or from any lesson or series of lessons on a religious subject, and such scholar shall be exempted accordingly, and a scholar shall not, by reason of any exemption from attending prayer or religious worship, or from any lesson or series of lessons on a religious subject, be deprived of any advantage or emolument in the School or out of the endowment of the Foundation to which he would otherwise have been entitled.

If the parent or guardian of, or person liable to maintain or having the actual custody of, any scholar who is about to attend the school, and who but for this clause could only be admitted as a boarder, desires the exemption of such scholar from attending prayer or religious worship, or from any lesson or series of lessons on a religious subject, but the persons in charge of the boarding houses of the School are not willing to allow such exemption, then it shall be the duty of the Governors to make proper provisions for enabling the scholar to attend the School and have such exemption as a day scholar, without being deprived of any advantage or emolument to which he would otherwise have been entitled.

If any teacher, in the course of other lessons at which any scholar exempted under this clause is in accordance with the ordinary rules of the School present, shall teach systematically and persistently any particular religious doctrine, from the teaching of which any exemption has been claimed as in this clause before provided, the Governors shall, on complaint made in writing to them by the parent, guardian, or person liable to maintain or having the actual custody of such scholar, hear the complainant, and enquire into the circumstances, and if the complaint is judged to be reasonable, make all proper provisions for remedying the matter complained of.

54.—The Governors may, if they think fit and the income at their disposal suffice for the purpose, agree with the Head Master for the formation of a fund in the nature of a Pension or Superannuation Fund, to be invested in the name of the Official Trustees of Charitable Funds, the main principles of such agreement being that the Head Master and the Governors respectively shall contribute yearly for a period of twenty years such sums as may be agreed on; that these contributions shall accumulate at compound interest; that in case the Head Master serves his office for such twenty years he shall on his retirement be entitled to the whole accumulated fund; that in case he retires earlier on account of permanent disability from illness he shall also be entitled to the whole of the same fund; that in all other cases he shall, on his ceasing to be Head Master, be entitled to the amount produced by his own contributions. If any question shall arise upon the construction or working of this provision, the same shall be referred by the Governors to the Charity Commissioners, whose decision thereon shall be final and conclusive.

55.—As soon as the state of the funds of the Foundation will admit, such a sum of Government stock belonging to the Foundation as will produce an income of 30l. a year for the time being, or as near that sum of stock as practicable, shall be placed to a separate account, entitled "Repairs and Improvements Fund." The income of such Fund shall be paid to the Governors and applied by them in ordinary repairs or improvements of property used for the purposes of the School, and if not wanted for that purpose shall be accumulated for the like purpose in any future year or years. Until the income of the Repairs and Improvements Fund amounts to 30l. a year it shall be made up to that amount out of the general income of the Foundation.

56.—Any income of the Foundation remaining in hand at the end of any year and not needed as a balance for meeting current expenses shall be treated as capital, and be invested in the name of the Official Trustees of Charitable Funds in trust for the Foundation in augmentation of its endowment.

57.—The Governors may receive any additional donations or endowments for the general purposes of the Foundation. They may also receive donations or endowments for any special objects connected with the Foundation which shall not be inconsistent with or calculated to impede the due working of the provisions of this Scheme. Any question arising upon this last point shall be referred to the Charity Commissioners for decision.

58.—Within the limits prescribed by this Scheme the Governors shall have full power from time to time to make regulations for the conduct of their business and for the management of the Foundation, and such regulations shall be binding on all persons affected thereby.

59.—Any question as to the regularity or the valadity of any proceedings under this Scheme, or as to the construction or application of any of the provisions of this Scheme, shall be referred by the Governors to the Charity Commissioners for their decision, and such decision shall be binding on the Governors and on all persons claiming under the Foundation who shall be affected by the question so decided.

60.—So far as relates to the Foundation, all jurisdiction of the Ordinary relating to or arising from the licensing of masters in any endowed school is hereby abolished.

61.—No person shall be disqualified for being a Master in the School by reason only of his not being, or not intending to be, in Holy Orders.

62.—From the date of this Scheme all rights and powers formerly reserved to, belonging to, claimed by, or capable of being exercised by, any person or body other than Her Majesty, as Visitor of the Foundation, and transferred to Her Majesty, and also any like rights or power vested in Her on the 2nd day of August, 1869, shall be exercised only through and by the Charity Commissioners for England and Wales.

63.—The Charity Commissioners may from time to time, in the exercise of their ordinary jurisdiction, frame Schemes for the alteration of any portions of this Scheme, provided that such Schemes be not inconsistent with anything contained in the Endowed Schools Act, 1869, and Amending Acts.

64.—Nothing in this Scheme shall affect any right which was in existence on the 13th day of May, 1875, relating to a chapel in Rivington, or any order of the Charity Commissioners now in force, so far as it makes provision for the discharge of any mortgage debt on any property of the Foundation, or for the replacement of any stock or money advanced out of the funds of the Foundation. From and after the date of this Scheme the Foundation shall for every purpose, except as in this Scheme provided, be administered and governed wholly and exclusively in accordance with the provisions of this Scheme, notwithstanding any former or other Scheme, Act of Parliament, Charter, or Letters Patent, Statute, or Instrument relating to the subject matter of this Scheme.

65.—The Governors shall cause this Scheme to be printed, and a copy to be given to every Governor, Head Master, and Assistant Master upon his entry into office, and copies may be sold at a reasonable price to all persons applying for the same.

66.—The date of this Scheme shall be the day on which Her Majesty by Order in Council declares Her approbation of it.

SCHEDULE OF PROPERTY.

	Description.	Extent.			Tenant or Person liable.	Gross yearly Income.		
		A.	R.	P.		£	s.	d.
1.	Freehold land and buildings, in the parish of Rivington, in the county of Lancaster, used for the purposes of the Rivington and Blackrod Grammar School.	7	3	36	—			
2.	Freehold land and buildings known as Spout House Farm, in the parish of Wheelton, near Chorley, in the County of Lancaster.	32	0	0	James Brindle	66	12	0
3.	Freehold land and buildings, known as Triggs Farm, in the parish of Wheelton, near Chorley, in the county of Lancaster.	34	2	23	Thomas Tootell	44	15	0
4.	Freehold land and buildings, known as Simpson Fold Farm, in the parish of Wheelton, near Chorley, in the county of Lancaster.	25	1	3	Ralph Emmott	45	0	0
5.	Freehold land and buildings, known as Flash Green Farm, in the parish of Wheelton, near Chorley, in the county of Lancaster.	26	2	36	George Smith	71	6	0
6.	Freehold land and buildings, known as Wheelton Lodge Farm, in the parish of Wheelton, near Chorley, in the county of Lancaster.	23	3	3	William Snape	37	16	0
7.	Freehold land and buildings, known as Wheelton House Farm, in the parish of Wheelton, near Chorley, in the county of Lancaster.	45	1	6	Wm. Burwell	90	0	0
8.	Freehold land and cottage, in the parish of Wheelton, near Chorley, in the county of Lancaster.				James Lowe	7	0	0
9.	Freehold land and buildings, known as Grave Oak Farm, in the parish of Bedford, in the county of Lancaster.	23	0	0	Henry & Sarah Wilkinson.	81	0	0
					Carried forward	443	10	0

Description.	Extent.			Tenant or Person liable.	Gross Yearly Income.		
	A.	R.	P.		£	s.	d.
				Brought forward	443	10	0
				L. Surtees	29	0	0
10. Freehold land and buildings, known as Hetton le Hole Farm, in the parish of Hetton le Hole, in the county of Durham.	33	0	0	Executors of Edmund Ashworth.	45	3	0
11. Freehold land and buildings, known as Shan Rose, in the parish of Turton, in the county of Lancaster.	22	3	0	Honourable F. Bowes Lyon (owner).	6	13	4
12. Rentcharge on Middleton's Land, in the parish of Silksworth, in the county of Durham.	—	—	—	Trustees of Robert Andrews (owners).	0	11	8
13. Rentcharge on Higher Knowle Farm, in the parish of Rivington, in the county of Lancaster.	—	—	—	Trustees of Robert Andrews & others (owners)	1	3	4
14. Rentcharge on Lower Knowle Farm, in the parish of Rivington, in the county of Lancaster.	—	—	—	Richard Shaw (owner)	0	5	0
15. Rentcharge on Grut Farm, in the parish of Rivington, in the county of Lancaster.	—	—	—	Representatives of R. S. T. Standish (owners).	0	13	4
16. Rentcharge on the Duxbury Estate, in the parish of Duxbury, in the county of Lancaster.	—	—	—	Trustees of the London Parochial Charities.	13	0	0
17. Two rentcharges, of £8 and £5 respectively, on property (formerly belonging to the parish of St. Sepulchre) in Lombard Street, London (John Holmes's gift.)	—	—	—				
18. A sum of £12 10s. 4d. New Consols standing to an Investment Account to which yearly sums of £6 to be paid out of the income of the Foundation and to be invested are to be transferred and accumulated to replace £156 8s. 5d. New Consols under order of the Charity Commissioners of the 10th September, 1889.	—	—	—	Official Trustees of Charitable Funds.	Dividends accumulating		
19. All other, if any, endowments of the Foundation.	—	—	—	—			
					539	19	8

NOTE.—The particulars in this Schedule, except as to the sum of New Consols, are put as ascertained or stated up to the 24th February, 1892; the particulars as to the said sum of New Consols are put as ascertained up to the 25th March, 1892.

Charity Commission,
6th May, 1892.

At a meeting of the Board held this day, at which there were present six Commissioners of whom one was the Chief Commissioner, this Scheme was approved and directed to be submitted to the Committee of Council on Education.

D. R. FEARON,
Secretary.

INDEX.

—:o:—

ABBOTT, John 124
    Accounts of Rivington Churchwardens 122-134
Ainsworth, John Henry 121
— Henry 122, 125
— Ra. 168
— Rev. Ralph 118
Anderton, Peter 118, 168
Anderton's Tenement 131
Anderton, Thomas 102, 167, 168
— Village of 11, 40
Andrew, John 168
Andrews, Mr. 125
— Robert . . . , 125, 127, 132, 133, 135
— — of Rivington Hall . 110, 138, 171
— Squire 125
Anglezark Mines 165
— Township and Rivington Church . 102
— Village of 40
Ashworth, James 144
Asshawe, Alice 13, 97
— Lawrence 13, 97
Astley, Samuel, preacher 167

BAIN, Isaac 139, 144
— James 144
— John 123, 127
Baryta, carbonate of 165
Bate, John 124
Beggars, endowed, their rights . . . 136
Beggar Charley 136
Berry, Andrew 144
"Black Boy" 43, 172
Blackburn, Rev. 109
"Black Lad" 43, 114, 134
— Origin of the name . . . 65
— New Ale House 144
Blackrod Grammar School 29
— Union with Rivington Grammar School 57-60
Blackrod Singers 133
Bleaching at Rivington 166
Boardman, Wright 139
Bourn, Rev. Samuel, his ordination . . 168
Bradley, John 168
Bradley, John, Old Rivington Schoolmaster, letter
  on School 150-152

Breers, Mr.	125
— Thomas, the elder	99
— Thomas, his claims to inheritance of Rivington Church and Churchyard	99
Briers, Mr.	124
Brindle's Tenement	124
Broadhurst —	102
— John, Charity	154
Bromilow, Thomas	127
Bromileys, John	124, 125
Bromley, Thomas	123
Brooke House	124, 131
Brookes, Richard of Matson	68
Brown Hill	127
Brown, George	124, 126
Brown's (George) House	126
Brown, Roger	143
Brownlow, Chris.	122
— George	122, 123, 128, 167
— James	118, 125, 168
— John	131
— Nicholas	122
— Richard	122, 125
— Thomas	122
Bueer, Martin	30
Burton, W.	131

CALAMY	115, 116
Carbonate of Baryta	165
Cates, Old-	143
Cawthorne, J. W., B.A.	46
Chair, Lord Willoughby's	74
Charley, The beggar	136
Charnley's (Rachael) Charity	154
Christopherson, John, D.D.	22
Churchwardens' Accounts	122-134
Churchwardens, Duties of	136
Churchwardens of Rivington	131, 133-4, 138-9, 143-4
Clayton, John, of Anglezark	104, 126, 144
— W.	138
Cocker, Moses, of Rivington	104, 122, 123
— Robert	124
"Comp., The," Rivington	139
Constables, requisitions to	137-138
Conventicle Act and Rivington	109
Crawford and Balcarres, Earl of	46, 57
Critchlor, Henry	124
Croft, Rev. R. C. W., M.A.	46
Crompton, Abram	171
— J. W.	35, 46
Crosses, Rivington	139
Crossfield, Rev. Thomas	110

DANDY, W.	133
Darbyshire, James	126
— John, (1693)	124
— John	168
— John, (1819)	138
Davenport, Henry	63, 73
Davies, B.	46

Dawson, George	170
Deane Church Singers	134
— Martyr, The	117
Dean Valley	161
Derbyshire, Bannister	134
Derby, Earl of	13
Devenport, Thomas	126
Devil's Dyke	164
Dewhurst, Robert, M.A., master of Rivington School	35
Diary of Lady Willoughby	75-95
Dissenters, The, and the Willoughbys	73
Dissenting Chapel at Rivington	168-9
Dixon, Rev. Joshua	109
Dob Lane Chapel	169
"Dow days"	43
"Dow ut Rivington"	43
Draper, Henry	68
Eccles, John, Death Sentence on	166
Eckersley, James	46
Education and Protestantism	31
— Sparsity of, in Lancashire	31
Egerton, Sir William, of Worsley	63, 72
Endowed School Commissioners' Scheme uniting Rivington and Blackrod Schools	46
Entwistle, Thomas	124
Fagius, Paulus	30
Fielding, John	102
Finch, John	124
Finch's Land	131
Finch, Peter	124
Fire at Rivington Church	143
Fisher, Rev. John	101, 109, 127, 132, 133, 139
Forest, ancient, of Rivington	9-11
Forest Laws	11
Foulds, village of	40, 182
Foster, John	134
— Thomas	125, 126, 129
Gardiner, Stephen, Bishop of Winchester	22-23
Garstang, James	130
Gaskell, Rev. W.	169
Gerrard, Roger	139, 142
Gilbert, Rev. J. S.	170
Gilpin, Bernard, M.A.	32
Gir Nest, Anglezarke	144
Governors of Rivington Grammar School	36
"Garnets," Anglezarke	131
Great House, Rivington	124, 144
Gridley, Albert	12
Green, Ralph	50
Greenhalgh, John	168
— Samuel	72
— W.	46
Grey, Rachel	121
— Wm.	121
"Grit"	126
Grundy, Thomas	126
Grut, Rivington	144

HALLIWELL, George	125
Halliwell, John	102
— Lawrence	72
— Village of	11
Halliwells, Old	138
Hamer, John	122, 124
Hampson, John - - 50, 101, 104, 123, 127, 128,	139
— Robert	123, 128
Handloom Weaving at Horwich	166
Hardy, Rev. Mr.	168
Hart, George, a confessor	35
— Thomas	133
Hatton, Rev. Richard, vicar of Deane	73
Hayes, Joseph	138, 143, 144
Heath Charnock	40
Heaton, Rev. Wm., M.A.	109, 121
— Village of	11
Hemshaw, village of, and Rivington Church	102
Heywood, Oliver, father of Nonconformist Divines	63
Hibbert, Rev. Nathaniel	169
Higher Knowl	124
Hindley, Rev. Thomas	109
Hodkinson, John	134
Hold Hall	138
Holt, Charles	139
— John	168
Hope, James	134
— John	138
Horrocks, John	142
— Will.	131, 134
Horewich ley	11
Horwich	40
— Church Built	74
— connection with the Willoughbys	73–75
— Handloom Weaving	166
— Singers	133, 134
Howarth, John	144
— Joseph	46
Hough, Richard	133
Hubbard, Rev. Cubit Boardman	170
Hutton, Rev. C. W. N., M.A.	46
INSTRUMENTAL Music at Rivington Church	133
Isherwood, John- - - 104, 122, 125, 134, 138,	139
Isherwoods	131
JACKSON, James	139
Jackson, Rev. James	109, 138
— his Eccentricities	172
Jenkins, Rev. John	169
Jepsons, in Anglezark	124
— in Rivington	124, 131
Johnson, Thos.	168
"Johnson's"	126
Justinian's Code	33
"KATE Taylor Robinson"	169
Kershaw, Richard	168
— John	132
— Jonathan	126
— W.	139

Kevan, J. 46
Kingsmills, John, Bishop Pilkington's
  Father-in-law 31
Kingsmills of Sidmanton, Hampshire . . 31
Knowle, Lower, Rivington 74

LATHAM, Henry - - - 123, 125, 127
  — Owd Dicky 123
Latham's Tenement - 126
Latham, Wm., clerk 131
  — Wm., of Rivington 104, 126, 129, 131, 132, 139
Lead Mines of Anglezark 165
Leaster, Richard 124
Lee Chapel 167
Lee, Joseph 126
  — Thomas 134
Leigh, John 124
  — Lord of Stoneleigh . . . 63, 72
  — Peter 124
  — Richard 124
Lester, Roger 126
Lever family 135
Lever, Robert, of Darcy Lever . . . 135
Lister Mill 139
Longworth, John 46
  — Joseph 138
  — Richard, M.A. 31
  — — ordination of . . 31
  — W. L. 46
Lord's Height 73, 74
Lords, Old 74
Lostock, village of 11
Low, Bennett 144
Lucas, Lawrence 127

MAGNALL, James 132
  Malthy, Henry Francis . . . 58
"Man and Scythe," Pilkington Crest . . 13
Marian persecutions 14
Marsh, George 117
Martineau, Dr., his visit to Rivington . 171
Mason, Adam 176
  — M. and A., Foxholes House . . 74
Mather, Thomas 124
Mayers, Rev. John 167
Methodist Raid on Rivington . . 171-2
Middleton, C. E. 46
  — Thomas 176
Miller, Wm. 127
Milnor, Henry 142
Mines of Anglezark 165
Montebegon, Rogerus de, Baron of Hornby 12
Moor Edge 124, 131
Moore's Almanac 134
Moss, W. 121
Morris, John 123, 124, 127
  — Obadiah, of Anglezark 104, 129, 131, 132
Morris's Rivington 139
Morris, Thomas 123, 124, 128
Musical services at Rivington Church . 133

NAYLOR, James		133
— New House, Rivington		124
Newton, Rev. S.		109, 115, 116
Nightingale, John		124, 127, 139
Noon Hill		117
Norcross, Rev. John		49, 101, 127
— — his will		49-50
— Thomas		132
Nuttal, Rauffe		115
OLD Coates		143
Oldham, Hugh, Bishop of Exeter		18
"Old Halliwells"		138
"Old Knows"		126
"Old Rachels"		143
"Old Wills"		126
PAKINGTON, (Pilkington) Alex.		12
Pass, John		122
Pass, W.		142
Pauls, C.A., B.Sc.		46
Paying the Shot		130
Pendlebury, Adam		124
— Richard		138
Peter, the beggar		136
Pigott, Rev. H. S.		110
Pike, The		145-9
Pilkington Crest		13
Pilkington, Dan		138
— E.		46
— family of		12-14
— Francis		36
— George		35
Pilkington, James, Bishop of Durham		14-39
— birth of		18
— descent from		18, 20
— educated at		14
— marriage to Alice Kingsmills		31
— marriage kept secret		31
— presented to vicarage of Kendal		14
— in exile		14
— — at Geneva		14
— — at Zurich and Basle		23
— — at Frankfort		24
— his letter to English Residents on the Continent		24
— one of the Compilers of the Book of Common Prayer		13
— his defence of the English Service		25
— return to England		14, 25
— elected master of St. John's, Cambridge		13
— consecrated Bishop of Durham		14
— criticism of Queen Elizabeth		15
— his strong Protestantism		15, 20-22
— his denunciation of Clerical indifference		15-16
— his sermon at St. Paul's Cross		16
— founder and endower of Old Grammar School at Rivington		17
— Grammar School endowments		32
— preached before Queen Elizabeth		26

Pilkington, James, Bishop of Durham (continued)
— his exposure of Elias, the
     "Manchester prophet" . . 26
— his book "Common Good" . . 26
— his letter to Earl of Leicester, 1564 - 27
— selected by Lord Mayor of London as
     one of the preachers of the Spital
     Sermons, but declined the honour 28
— a commissioner of the University of
     Cambridge 30
— select preacher before the University
     of Cambridge . . . 30
— preaches funeral sermon on Martin
     Bucer and Paulus Fagius . . 31
— his death 17
— his will 35
Pilkington, John 35
— Leonard, D.D. 26, 35
— Margaret 35, 169
Pilkington Motto 13
Pilkington, Richard, second son of Sir Roger
     Pilkington 13
— Richard, Lord of Manor of Pilkington,
     father of Bishop of
     Pilkington . . 13, 18, 97, 98, 101
— Samuel 134
— Sir Roger, Lord of Pilkington . 13
— Sir Thomas 13
— W. 50
Pilkingtons, The, and the Civil War . . . 36
Pimbley, Joseph 133
Plague, The great, of 1551 27
Poor, the laws relating to 136
Poor, rights of 136
Presbyterian Chapel, Rivington . . . 172-3
Protestantism and Education . . . 31
Psalmody, teaching of 138
Punishments at School 45

RACECOURSE, The 73
   Rachels, Old 143
Rainfall at Rivington 165-6
Rawcliffe, H. 46-57
Rawlins, Rev John 169
— Thomas 169
Reformation, The, in Lancashire . . 31-32
Reynolds, Thomas 124
Ridgway Arms 18
— Joseph, Ridgmont . . . 18, 74
Ritson, Rev. W., M.A. . . . 46, 103, 109
Rigby, Charles 139
Rivington, variations in spelling . . . 7
— its geology 8
— its etemology 9
— its early inhabitants . . . 9
— dependency of Barony of
     Manchester 12
— and the Act of Uniformity . 109, 115, 116
— and the Conventicle Act . . 109
— parochial chapelry of . . 126, 127, 129
— Vestry meeting, July 4th, 1774 . 127

Rivington, public meetings of
      inhabitants - - 125, 128, 129, 131
  — singers - - - - 133
Rivington Waterworks - - - 157-9
  — — description of reservoirs - - 158
  — — memorandum of agreement
        between Christopher Shaw
        and Liverpool Corporation - 160
Rivington Hall - - - - - 18
  — — description of - - - 35
  — — old one pulled down - - 35
  — — new one built - - - 35-36
Rivington Chapel - - - - 99, 118, 167
  — — accommodation of - - 169
  — — manse - - - 171
  — — Library - - - 171
  — — list of ministers - - 169-70
  — — Schoolroom - - - 171
  — — turned Unitarian - - 173
Rivington Church, builder of - - 13, 97-99
  — — and churchyard, claim to
        inheritance of - - 99
  — — rebuilt - - - 101-102
  — — churchwardens - - 131-144
  — — churchwardens' accounts 122-134
  — — and the marriage service - 102
  — — unique privileges - - 102
  — — the curate - - 102-103
  — — endowments - - 102
  — — inventory of goods in 1552 103
  — — no patron saint - - 103
  — — charter of - - 105-108
  — — and Grammar School - 105
  — — clergy of, list of - 109
  — — tablets and brasses in church 115-116
  — — music at - - 133
  — — instrumental music at - 133
  — — singers paid - - 133
  — — books in church chest - 143
  — — parsonage, particulars of - 143
  — — stipend of minister - 143
  — — incendiary fire at church - 143
Rivington Grammar School - - 17, 29, 32, 114
  — endowments of - - - 32, 140
  — Queen Elizabeth letters patent - 32
  — charter of foundation of - 32, 52, 56
  — governors of, chosen from six townships 32
  — master's salary - - - 32
  — usher's salary - - - 32
  — form of prayers for use in school - 32-33
  — statutes of the school - 32, 36 39
  — Bishop Pilkington's will - - 35
  — nomination and appointment of
      Governors - - - 40
  — Qualification for a Governor - 40
  — Oath taken by a Governor - - 41
  — duties of a Governor - - 42
  — headmasters - - - 43
  — school punishments - - 45
  — cost of new school - - 46
  — opening of new school in 1882 - - 46

Rivington Grammar School (continued)
- course of study and exhibitions - 47-48
- examination of school - 48, 51, 52
- scheme for conjoining Blackrod and Rivington schools - 57-60
- and church - 105
- dispute as to appointment of Samuel Waring to head mastership - 132
- popular control of endowments ceased - 140
- benefaction fund - 141-2
- trustees of, in 1840 - 142
- action of governors criticised by Thos. Middleton and Adam Mason - 174-6
- charity scheme of 1889 - 152-6
- — — 1893 - 178-196

Rivington lane - 18
Rivington, Thos. - 167
Rivington Pike - 145, 149
Robberds, Rev. C. W. - 170
— John Gooch - 170
Robinson, Kate Taylor - 169
Roscoe, Baxter - 65, 73
Roscoe's Tenement - 126, 139
Rothwell, Edward - 144
-- Peter - 133
— Ralph, of Brownlow Fold - 49
— Rev. James - 117, 169
— Thomas, of Haigh - 72
Rowlinson, Rev. W. - 169
Rumworth, village of - 11
Ryder, W. - 144

SCHOOL punishments - 45
Sefton, John - 124
Sentinel Hill - 140
Sharples township and Rivington Church - 102
Sharples, Wm. - 124
Shaw's Charity, value of - 140, 153
Shaw, Charles - 73, 131, 134, 138
— family of - 144
— George - 102, 114
Shaw's House - 126
Shaw, James - 73, 131
— John, of Anglezark, bequests of - 142
— John, Chapel Warden for Jephson's - 131
— John, of Shaw Place - 65, 73, 115, 142
-- Lawrence - 114, 115
— Mrs., of Pilkington's - 131
— Peter - 97
Shaw Place - 65, 96, 97
— origin of name - 97
Shaw, Richard - 73
Shaws of Rivington - 73
Shaw, Thomas - 35
Simm, James - 122, 123, 124, 125, 127
— John - 124
— John, the incendiary - 143
— Richard - 99
— Roger - 122
Smelting furnaces, remains of - 165
Smith, Andrew - 57

Smith, Nathan 142
— Thomas 126
— W. 144
— Zachariah 121
Snape, Richard 124
Spencer, R. O. 46
Spokesman of Rivington Grammar School
    Governors 36
Squire, Rev. George, M.A. 46
Standish, Sir Frank, Bart. 132
Stocks at Rivington 130
Stock's pad, Horwich 131
Stone House, Anglezark 124
Stone's House 126
Swift, Mr. 35
Survey of 1650 115
Sutcliffe, Rev. T. 57, 109
— sketch of 110
— death and funeral sermon . 110-113
Sweetlove, Edm. 122, 123, 127
— W. H. 124

TAYLOR, Wm. 144
    Tebay, Rev. Septimus 58
Thompson, Rev. Samuel 170
Thropp, Roger 124
Turner, Mr., Anglezark 124
— Rev. John 118, 169-70
— Rev. W. 118, 134

UNITARIAN Chapel, Rivington . . 115, 173
    Unsworth, John 8, 46
Unsworth, Thomas 138
Upholland, religious house of . . . 19

VAUX, Lawrence, native of Blackrod, Warden
    of Manchester 29
Village Customs 130

WADDINGTON, John 129
    Waddington, Rev. John . . . 109
Walkden, John 133-134
Walker, Parson 118
— Rev. John . . . 109, 116-119, 168
Walmsley, Nicholas of Preston . . . 104
Walton, James, of Heath Charnock . . 73
"Wards" 131, 134
Waring, Samuel, dispute as to his appointment
    to headmastership of Rivington Grammar
    School 132
Waterfall, The 161
Weathercock for Church 132
Wells, Rev. G. H. 169
Welsh, Rev. W. 101, 104, 109
— his resignation of Rivington Chapel 101
Whalley, religious house of . . . 19
Whalley, Thomas 124
Whewell, Edward 133
Whittall (Whittle), Thomas, of Horwich . 65, 71, 72
Whittaker, Rev. J., M.A. 18
Widdows, E. 46

Wilcocks, John	131, 132
Wild, W.	132
Wilding, Thomas	58
Will of Rev John Norcross	49–50
William Fitz William	12
Williamson, T	46
Willis, General	118
Willoughbys of Parham or Parnham, Family of	62–75
Willoughby peerage, history of	67–72
Willoughbys, connection with Horwich	73–75
Willoughby epitaph in Chapel at Rivington	63–65
Willoughby, Hon. Hugh, 15th Baron of Parnham	62, 104, 126
— death of, and burial	75
Willoughbys, The, and the Dissenters	73, 168
Willoughby's (Lord) chair	74
Willoughby, Lady, her diary	75–95
Wilson, John	124, 142
— Joseph	104
— Lee	101
— Thomas	131
Winter Hill, Rivington	109, 117
Withering, Dr.	165
Witherite	165
Woodcock, John	124
Woods, Parson	118
— W.	143
Worsley, James	124, 168

www.ingramcontent.com/pod-product-compliance
Lightning Source LLC
Chambersburg PA
CBHW020912230426
43666CB00008B/1428